Bloom

Copyright © 2021 by Red Penguin Books

Editor Nika Jordan Rose

All rights reserved

Published by Red Penguin Books

Bellerose Village, New York

ISBN

Print 978-1-63777-056-6

Digital 978-1-63777-057-3

Library of Congress Control Number: 2021909441

No part of this volume may be reproduced in any form or by any electronic or mechanical means, including information storage and retrieval systems, without written permission from the author, except for the use of brief quotations in a book review.

CONTACT US

For general inquiries, write to
bloomlitmagazine@gmail.com

SUBMISSIONS

If you'd like to contribute, email us at
bloomlitmagazine@gmail.com

SPONSORS

To enquire about advertising or sponsorships,
get in touch at stephanie@redpenguinbooks.com

CONTRIBUTORS

Ed Ahern
Leigh Alder
Ashrena Ali
Marina Antropow Cramer
Isabelle Avola
Joe Baumann
Kristina Carpenter
Shevaun Cavanaugh Kastl
Debbie De Louise
Ramesh Dohan
Roy Duffield
Kate E Lore
Elana Gomel
John Grey
J Hirtle
Amanda Hurley
Sejo Jose
Jane Killingbeck

Catherine Kim
Allan Lake
Brandy Lane
Tiffany Lindfield
Dan Mariani
Brandon Marlon
J.S. Mannino
Jill Ocone
Lisa Rosenblatt
Carl Scharwath
Evren Kadir Sezgin
Evelyn Sharenov
Linda Trott Dickman
Benedetto Varotta
A. O. Wallat
Allison Whittenberg
Jenna Zeihen
煦 (Susie Zhu)

No part of this publication may be reproduced, distributed, or transmitted in any form or by any means, including photocopying, or other electronic or mechanical methods, without the prior written permission of the editor.

from the editor...

Welcome to Bloom, the literary magazine dedicated to the growth of the emerging (or re-emerging) author! We are delighted to share our second issue with you. In the pages ahead you'll find work by writers, both emerging and established, that pushes against the limitations of form. It is our hope that Bloom will continue to act as a virtual "playground" for writers to explore their work without restriction, try their hand at something new, and/or finally submit that piece they thought couldn't quite "fit" anywhere. Once again, our call for exciting original work was met! I hope that you read through this issue with intention and leave with a fire burning within you to write something new, something never thought you would or could writer, something that expands you, and most importantly, leads to your growth as an author. We look forward to seeing that work in our next edition. Until then, enjoy!

Nika Rose

an interview

USA Today bestselling author Joanne Rock has written over one hundred books, most recently focusing on sexy contemporary romance and small-town family sagas. She enjoys romance for prioritizing relationships and placing emphasis on personal happiness. A frequent speaker at regional and national writing conferences, she enjoys giving back to the writing community that nurtured and inspired her early career. Joanne has a Master's degree in Literature from the University of Louisville and a lifelong love of books.

Joanne Rock - USA Today Bestselling Author
https://www.joannerock.com/
https://www.facebook.com/JoanneRockAuthor
Twitter: @JoanneRock6
Instagram: @joannerock6

An Interview with Joanne Rock
By Bloom Editor Nika Rose

Nika: I'd love to hear about your journey with creativity as a young person and the media you connected to.

Joanne: I started out always enjoying writing. I loved reading. I think that's common for writers; that they're just hardcore readers and book fans from a very young age. Even in high school, English teachers would say, "You're such a gifted writer." To me, it always seemed easy. I thought, "That's just a thing. It's just writing." It felt very natural. It didn't occur to me to do something with it until I went to college for Public Relations. I thought "I'm a people person. I want to take people out for dinner on a company credit card." You know, the kind of crazy things you come up with at 18 and think, "This would be a good life." I was in the job for about a year and I realized it wasn't fun having a company credit card if you're going out to dinner with clients and not your friends. It was just different than what I'd envisioned. I still loved books. I couldn't read enough. I wanted to crawl inside of a book, to find a way to enjoy them even more. It hit me- that's writing. I decided to get my master's in English and study literature, which is what I'd always loved, and I'd approach a career that way. To do what I already knew I enjoyed. I started writing a book on the first day of graduate school. I was sitting on campus and I thought that was a very graduate student thing to do; to sit and start writing a book. I probably set that aside the minute I got into a class and thought, "Man, this is going to be a lot of work." But it started the dream right then and there. I started to want to write romance as I began reading a lot of it in graduate school as a brain cleanse between the really hard literary-critical theory. After I untwined those three paragraph-long sentences, I'd just want to read a romance. To just read text that I could understand well. It was really escapist. I quickly decided that that quality was like a magic superpower. To be able to write a story that's so transporting that we forget everything else. I thought, "I'd love to be able to do that." I feel like that's what I've been working toward my whole career. I don't know if I've performed it as well as other people but I'm constantly striving. That's what I want to do.

N: At that point was writing your full-time priority or were you still dabbling in other income sources?

J: I had an assistantship. So I was teaching at the same time that I went to graduate school. I really enjoyed that too, enjoying books with other people. Talking about books is a great way to learn. I've always enjoyed teaching writing and film, just teaching story and talking about story. I've frequently done that part-time, even once I'd sold books. I've found it's a nice companion to writing. I was also doing freelance writing, writing human interest stories. I was writing that way while I dreamed about writing a book.

N: How do you balance writing for joy with the business side of writing?

J: It's hard. It's a career-long battle to be focused and disciplined. It's a creative field. Going into something that's a passion and making it a money-making enterprise is difficult to balance. That's always a struggle. You have to find ways to continue what you really love about it and still be prolific and productive and have it support you. It can be a love/hate relationship some days. I try to just set aside a block of time and decide in that time I'm working on my personal interests, what I'm passionate about. That's the time for my book, nothing else. I think that's very important. Back then it was the BICHOK acronym (butt in chair, hands on keyboard.) I forgot who came up with that but I really bought into that whole idea. If I just sit my butt there, words must happen. Since then I've learned that a lot of writing doesn't take place in the chair. Most of it takes place wandering around, thinking. Writing doesn't look like you're working, at least the hardest part of it, it looks like you're daydreaming. The actual crafting of text, putting words on paper, I've always found that a little bit easier. It's coming up with the story that's the hard part for me. To ensure I'm productive I either set an amount of time every week I need to spend writing or a page count that I have to produce. I'm really goal-oriented so depending on where I'm at in the process the numbers change. When you're first starting you can't really expect much of yourself because you're learning everything. You write more pages but you delete everything and redo it. It's confusing when you're first starting out. But I'd say I've continued to always have that number of hours or pages that I want to get done. That's very focusing for me. I can move on and do other things once I get X accomplished.

N: I want to circle back to something you said about your love for teaching story. At this point in your career, having written and read as many books as you have, what have you learned about crafting story? What are the key elements you're plotting out?

J: I've gotten much better at character growth. I'd say the emotional component has always been a hard facet for me. That's what I struggle with most; how does the story, how does the love relationship teach them so that they can do something at the end that they couldn't at the beginning. How do they grow? I've worked hard on that my entire career. It's one of the most difficult facets of storytelling. I love the sexy, made-for-screen parts, the meet-cute. I love to think of those parts. That's never been hard for me. I enjoy that tremendously. The big kind of romantic, sweeping ending- that's fun. The quieter emotional story that's underneath all of that, that's what readers are there for. It's not just the big exciting things. It's the emotional growth, the battles they go through. It's how they change, how they grow, how they become better people that we're really there for. I still work on that. I put a lot of thought into that. I'd like to think I've gotten better. You get better with all of your elements but you forget things that you've learned and you relearn them. You get inspired by other people as you grow. I've learned that your process evolves all the time. Every few years I do something different and mix it up. I think that's actually very healthy. Some writers worry about that. Worry that a book is coming to them so differently than the last one. They're all very different beasts. You just need to try to follow them. At least that's what I've found.

N: Is there a specific author that you've been inspired by?

J: I've always been inspired by my friend, Catherine Mann. She's my critique partner and she's been an inspiration since day one. I think because I work so closely with her and I get to see her creative process. You don't get to do that with many people. I feel very lucky to see how she creates story, how she talks through it, the types of things she thinks about as she's coming up with a story. That's really useful. She has a theatre background. She thinks so visually because of it. Early on that helped me think about my stories differently. What are they doing? If I was going to make it a screenplay, what could actually be shown? In romance, it's narrative and feeling and thinking. None of that would make it to the screen or stage if I was to show this. It really helped me to reframe what I was doing. I still love the internal thought and I love when other writers do it. They say to work with people who complement you and do something different. I think that's how she has really complemented me and my process. She drives me to give readers more of that visual experience. And the auditory, what you hear, the dialogue, the back and forth that you'd listen to as you watch a play or film.

N: Could you tell me about how your critique partnership works? How often do you check in? What do you look for?

J: We started working together before either of us had sold a book. I think it's helpful to work with someone who's at about your same level. I think sometimes people will want to search for someone who knows everything and can give you the answers but there's something great about finding out the answers with someone else, going through the whole process with someone else. They're right where you are. There was a pushing each other forward. If she learned something, she shared it. She explained it to me. If I figured something out, I called her and said, "Guess what? This was such a lightbulb moment for me!" That was really helpful. As we found our rhythm, we started to exchange every three chapters. I would read her first three chapters, she'd read my first three chapters, and we'd move on to the next batch. Now we read every chapter. It's a little bit quicker. As the pace of life is more frenetic, you can read one chapter pretty quickly and give feedback. We look at both the big picture and the ticky-tacky. If I see typos, I fix typos. But she doesn't count on me to fix her typos. She counts on me to say, "Hey! You forgot your growth," or "Hey! Your character is acting out of character. I thought he was this because of this in his backstory and now he's behaving this way." Anything that, as a reader, I feel is inconsistent I will point out to her and vice versa. I write for Harlequin Desire. It's the world of the American elite. So if I have too much gritty background and haven't shown the wealthy world people want, she'll say, "You need some glitz and glam. Get the five senses in there, Joanne!" She shows me innumerable things that she feels like I'm not doing in my manuscript and vice versa. The nice thing about a long relationship like that is that I know she always has my best interest at heart. I never have to worry that she hates my book, which is a huge fear when you're beginning a critique relationship. Some people will tear apart your book or some people are looking for different things, for a different relationship. It's very difficult to find someone who speaks your language and that you can get comfortable with. It just takes time and trying out different partnerships to see who's a good fit for you. It's so very worth it in the end if you can develop that kind of relationship.

N: Do you think the romance genre has something to offer at this particular moment in our culture?

J: So much. I've always thought that romance has a lot to offer. One of the best things about it, and I've always found this, is that it leaves me feeling hopeful. It's an optimistic genre. Things work out. There's a happy ending. I can't tell you how much more I need that now than what I needed even 20 years ago. I need that sense that it can work out, that you can resolve your problems. That's a message, no matter where the story goes, that I crave. I feel like I can't soak that up enough right now. Beyond that, in a deeper way, I think romance teaches us to address our problems. People that don't read romance have this sense of romance as all wine and roses. They think it's going on dates and being happy. But no, there's a huge problem, a conflict. You're working through a conflict with another person and you're also working out conflicts with yourself. It's not really about the conflict with the other person, so much of it is internal. They can't trust. They had this hard relationship. They were divorced. Something in their backstory makes them not able to connect with somebody. So it's working on those problems, personally. I think romance can be very instructive. It can teach you how to question yourself, to see your own biases, to respect what another person has to offer. It teaches you that sometimes when a partner says something cutting, it's not about you. It's self-directed. It's a cynicism. It teaches you to see that dual perspective. I think that makes you more empathetic. I could go on all day. I just think there's so much emotional value in romance.

Ghost Writer
Ramesh Dohan

I have rarely felt
Such a permanent failure
Intact and sweet smelling
The metaphor of a heart
Takes turn with
Sometimes, I must be allowed to leave you
Forgetting the plot is the best
For I am cold here
On the warm side of the glass

Upcountry
Brandon Marlon

Inland wayfarers halt at a ramshackle bivouac
off the beaten track by the vermeil light
of sunup for last-minute victuals
as they ready to surmount hurdles,
their eyes aloft toward the summit distant
and neutral to their quest, at best.

They espy just ahead amid cacti
the bleached bones of carcasses
picked clean by vulturous scavengers,
beneficiaries of time and chance.

Smoke from breakfast fires spirals
afar into the plain, masking chaparral
and startling patterned rattlers
from hidden dens onto the warmth
of earth cracked and peeling.

Equipped to ascend, the living know
well how impartial wilderness remains
toward civilization's refugees
who place themselves at the mercy
of forces amoral and untamed;
yet life ever seeks other life,
undaunted by the pitfalls and perils
nested amid nature wild and awaiting.

Lag
Allison Whittenberg

When you realize,
'Please return the library books
They're on the table'
As her last words
Balances every "I love you" she'd given

Instead of goodbye
The incessant, familiarity of instruction
the sum
                                        of my mother

The Time of Day
Ed Ahern

aA widow walks by my house each day
in syncopation with the mailman.
She had also lost a daughter,
but what is gone is carried deep,
for she always smiles and stops to chat.
We exchange perhaps two hundred words
about weather and children and neighbors,
but never about the death and absence
so twined into our daily living,
and the knitting we do to cope.
We sense with tacit understanding
that our inanities give unsaid comfort
to our silenced fears and grief.

THE BEAUTY PAIN
John Grey

Bees waltz on open flowerheads.
Barbaric nippers - no, honeyed buzz.
What can win tears but the praise of nettles.
And poison ivy, like Daphnis, is a shepherd
in the weeds, a flautist in the wind.
A countryside of pain releases the passion.
More genuine than happiness.
A cut of razor leaves. A bullying ants nest.
Mosquito squadron. Wild rose thorns.
A sting in April is a dance in May.

River Dance
Linda Trott Dickman

For all those who swim upstream

We move toward the light
From the very beginning,
Swimming, in a dark pool
Upstream is what we do.

Rising from darkness into starkness.
Recoiling from the light at first
Then, resting in it, sleeping through it.

We swim from salt to brackish to fresh to living
water. Relentless,
stopping on the gravel, eggs strewn like pearls
pushing through placenta, ever moving.

Tides lave over us, storms move us,
falls force us backward.
Sometimes, into completely different streams,
washed from all we know.
Still striving, thriving,
building muscle - from gravel, up solid rock.
Moving, always drawn to reach for the impossible.

Sparkling, endangered, in pain,
rising in leaps of faith
flying toward the One
who made the surge to life eternal
in this river
leave it all behind
in the twinkling of an eye.

A POEM NEVER READ
Carl Scharwath

My words
 Composed and forgotten.
 Created like
 A dewdrop
 That vanishes
 In the primordial
Morning
Sunshine.
 Evolving into
The loudest silence
 Never heard…

Air and Other Foreign Bodies
Isabelle Avola

The fair noon sun
blooms on me
that effervescent red
hid under eyelids, only I can see.
To visit the shade
safe under sun
To ride this wave,
the pulse it leaves
underneath my tongue
of words unsaid
and actions undone
honestly,
honesty weighs a tonne.

Daddy, oh
(for Lawrence F)
Allan Lake

If your father is messing-inaction
you look round for replacement but
that's your secret even you don't know.
Dad: a beaten conundrum, a goldfish
that forsakes water in favour of booze.
Son – not a reflective moon – alters course,
makes tracks in deep space or sea,
learning to navigate, searching for real gold
or god and despite the inherited folly,
trips into a riptide of lucky duck water,
finds himself in the wake of a whale
and realises it's a wholly new brand
of buoyant Daddy. So long, all
that's familiar, wasn't really that good
to know you. Whale's water-tight advice?
Remember everything except how to swim
back to land and create fluid language
any fish can understand.

In Which We Were Hinged
Ashrena Ali

You came to me, naturally, like waves chasing
the shore. Finally, what felt like sending a hundred-thousand
Morse codes, I found the right sequence
hidden in an algorithm written
only for the stars; fastened together by virtual letters.
You do this thing to me where you blend touch,
soft words; fill the gaps within my chest.
I am falling; love is a kind of falling. Not in the crumbling,
sinking way; in the way the sun gracefully descends
into the stirring sea, both meeting on the axis of the world
no longer living like a fragment; here I only connect to you.

The Teeth at the Edge of the World
Kristina Carpenter

Rows of white that dot the sky
in long, slow march across the horizon—
What are they?
Too still to be clouds.
Too far to be flowers
or orchards of apple trees in spring.
Too round to be peaks of glistening snow
and too even, too white,
Gnawing at the sky, the grass, the trees,
Biting them off from our vision.
What is there, where the white rows stand?
Mountain? Sky? Sea?
Or nothing:
An abyss—
a night without moon when clouds obscure the pin-prick stars
or caverns where the blind fish swim.
An emptiness—
like what you feel when the curtain falls that final time
or the book is shut, the dream pops.
Something gnaws at you, at the sky and the trees.
The teeth at the edge of the world.

Grounded
Roy Duffield

                                                                  change

to

                    bound

              less

                               far

                         They are

                             stars.
                  I look to the
You're down to earth, your feet on the ground, while

Sun and Moon
Brandy Lane
from her book <u>Where Beautiful Loves</u>

If I could

capture the **sunshine**,
I would place it outside your window...
to brighten your days and disposition.

As far as the **moon**?
I'd put a pull chain on it so you could
turn it off when you wanted to see

all of the **stars**...
and turn it on

whenever you felt alone at **night**.
You could adjust it waxing or waning,
so you could take a midnight stroll,

or sit quietly next to your **true love**
and watch it move across the night sky.

Leaving her behind.
Jenna Zeihen

A new year's day filled with mourning
over more time I could've had
if my body wasn't set
on being shattered.
They stare at me like fire froze.
A spring flower in the hands of January.
The doctor walks away.
Magic has a cost.
Hopeful remedies have
consequences.
A battle where you blame them for not knowing
and yourself for not trying a little bit harder.
The underscore to it all, a song of disbelief.
No one knowing what it's like
to leave the girl I built behind.
It feels never-ending...
Nevermind.

Rewilders
Brandon Marlon

Limpid views dissipate mists
dimming the minds of observers
beholding the unrelenting panorama
of apple orchards and lavender farms,
their thoughts harking back
to prior epochs in an appended land
lush with waterfalls and rainforests.
Humble in gait and mien, they trek
wide-eyed amid fern labyrinths,
listening for a susurrus latent if not patent,
the subtilized pulse of space and time.
They surpass chasms toward rugged highlands
where tessellated pavements await;
there they admire the moment,
sighing aloft to yellow wattlebirds
the expiating pangs of heirs
keen to annul the trespasses of forebears
once unsure whether to explore or exploit.
By the bay they encounter aborigines
intent on salmon and rockweed,
sharing gratitude for outback blessings,
the largesse warmly conferred on renewers
of bonds fondly remembered.

Gleaning the Attic
Ed Ahern

The purgatory of my possessions
reproaches me from the jumbled attic.
Dusty sleeping bags and thermal wear
cached for trips no longer taken.
Books on fishing and philosophy
long unnibbled except by paper lice.
An oversized, silver-plated tea service,
a present from a long-gone aunt,
blackened from never once being used.
Phonograph records from a dead mother
not played in several decades.
A concretion of things once treasured,
lacking any present grace or purpose,
hoping to be redeemed by new owners.

YOUR REGULAR POETRY PROGRAMMING HAS BEEN DELAYED
John Grey

Early morning,
I am in a strange new city,
dying for that caffeine rush,
and I can't find a Starbucks.

I wander street after street
but there's no sign of
that green and white mermaid,
the woman I'd surely fall
in love with
if I was ever a corporate logo.

I ask a local
and he merely shrugs his shoulders.
"Starbucks? Never heard of them."

I promise myself
never to go somewhere
without getting a heads up beforehand
on the nearest Starbucks location.

At least, I would promise myself
if my head wasn't such a fog,
if my bloodstream
could get out of first gear,
if my legs didn't have
to do all this walking
without help from my brain.

I apologize
if this sounds more like
an advertisement
than a poem.

But I write all my poems
in Starbucks.
I don't know what this is.

Sunday Morning
Carl Scharwarth

reasoning about my place in the future to arrive
I am anonymous and have forgotten myself
how far back do we journey to find our new beginning?

One Sunday
Ashrena Ali

Tonight, you're alone in this room
empty of me, save for my smell
that's in it. The sheets are full of
stains still damp from our love residue
or the cat's licking of his fur.
Where I am, I linger over:
your name in my head, the vowels
like whispering moans; the sheets rise
lightly. You know the slant of my limbs
the bow in my back –
Only then did I feel time slip
from my fingers. I watched the cars
pass on Memphis Street like a mystic flurry.
I knew then I could not leave you,
or find anyone I would love more.

AA (Artist Anonymous)
Allison Whittenberg

  Loud music filled the room, making it hard to hear anything else. Pass the cappuccino.
  I had another brain surge this morning – it wasn't a pretty feeling. Then it all started coming back to me in big red chunks.
  I could feel it happening, damnit, and I got all whacked and surrealistic, reverting back to me from myself. Contemptible precariousness surfacing once more and, if I could, I would take a whip and chair out to my imagination and kill it -- dead.
  But the music of my voice moved through my ears mellifluously, making my senses yield.
  Hadn't I gone to this movie before?
  It won't go away this satanic appendage, and I keep biting my hide, searching for metaphysical fleas.
  The right side of my brain keeps hurting. Ghost pains?
  A Bogus façade peels like sunburn.
  And I do feel optimistic now and then (more then).
  Is there no refuge where I might towel off, emotionally?
  It's a fate worse than life.
  Pass the cappuccino.

Spirals
Kristina Carpenter

"Those who do not learn from history are doomed to repeat it."
-George Santayana

Spiraling—
whirlpools of swirling water,
tornadoes, swirling air,
spiral, repeat—
rhythmically, continuously
constant.
How many times does the water,
the air, traverse the same point,
same line, same space, it once
traveled before?
Can we get back a moment,
frozen in the past, thawed and
restored to relive and re-grasp,
re-created, rejuvenated
again?
Lightning strikes, fires burn
erratic shapes into my
mind, but water swirls and air
whirls over and over,
constant.
How many times does one particle
of oxygen, hydrogen dioxide,
occupy that same place in space
as it did moments ago?
But even if velocity is
constant,
if conditions are consistent,
what are the chances,
even though the wind bends
in mighty gusts that circle,
spiral, twist,
that even this, that anything
ever exists,
just for a moment, anywhere
it did before?

Backyard Dreams
Ramesh Dohan

The front door wide open
to a sky of windblown herons, pewter
wings bent back
the acre of grass is a sleeping
swarm of locusts
Nina Simone sings
In the next room without a body
I am against the wall, dream-headed
I turned the family portrait facedown
When he was on me
What he calls me is not my name
And I love it
Damask chair beside the lion claw tub
Where I pretended to drown

Seasoned Moments
Ed Ahern

Old Age is pointillism of experience
Vibrant on a graying canvas
Moments of self-illumination
Shining like a Russian icon
Atop drab robes.
The weathered revel in instants

THE LOVER
John Grey

I was in love from the beginning.
Inside the womb's fleshy cathedral,
outside in the holy temples of the sun.

At birth, I was an ode quickly filling with lines.
At two, I knew the words to sell the crowd
on what I was feeling my way through.

By eight, I dreamed the future intact.
At twelve, I looked up at the days to come
from the ground level of acne and adoration.

By fifteen, I heard the same thing in girls
as I did in trees and birdsong.
At seventeen, the same could be said for galaxies.

I was twenty, and everything I so wanted to compare
was incomparable.
I wrote poems, to steady my hand mostly.

All through the next decade,
I fell for this one and that one,
and maybe misery most of all.

Until, that is, at thirty, I came upon
this dead ringer for permanence,
and we moved in together.

I was in love with the end of so much
and its alter ego, what was beginning.
And I've been pleased and a little relieved

that my love works as well in focus
as it did in all that scattered objectifying of my youth.
I feel confident enough now to be loving

up to, but not including, death,
For death has always been the spoiler.
And life, of course, is what spoils it for me.

Fortunate for Love
Ashrena Ali

I've been in love several times before
never knowing if it was the last love.
I should mention I've been in love with:
places, unknown
faces, or things – steaming coffee at 8am, the smell
of peppermint, shaved legs under
clean linen – I imagine love in the world began
like this. Yes, I have been in love before. But you,
you, and only you I have been
fortunate enough to meet and not miss.

What If We Felt the Invisible
Kristina Carpenter

What if we felt the invisible,
the way we feel the wind in giant gusts
that throw our hair about our heads like seaweed
when winds stir up the water
in waves that heave and surge breathlessly?
Is that what anticipation looks like?
Or would it scream across the storm-wrecked earth
in little trembles after the first quake
while the survivors wait to see if
the first great tremor will be the last
or just omen of greater loss to come.
The way a man at the airport terminal
waits, looking from head to head and eye
to eye, and even when the minutes
tick by keeps waiting, looking, expecting.
And now hate and love and grief—
to touch them, hold them in our hands,
hear them, see them, study under microscope?
Would hate look like a tide, washing back and
forth, rising, ebbing with the day and cycle
of the moon? Or love a trembling glass so
smooth and fragile, beautiful but cold?
What if we could feel the invisible
things, a child neglected, kept inside from
school, from friends, from family,
overlooked by teachers, judges,
social workers who promised to protect?
Would it feel like a rock tied
to your back, a constant pressure, hard
and cold, each step, each time you sit and
stand a labor of Herculean strain?
Is to see to understand, to feel to
create a bond between the tangible
and the things we never could touch?
How to go back to the tangible things,
to extract them from nuances, from
fears? The eyes show the soul but
who has seen it? I see in your eyes your
soul, distorted, but if your soul took shape,
what else would I see, feel?
What if we could feel the invisible?
Would we feel more pain or less?

Agents of Entropy
J.S. Mannino

From the order at the origin
To utter chaos within a blink
The ruthless march of time has begun
Before there were even minds to think

From the singularity burst
A quantum of the infinite
Hurtling helplessly through spacetime
Ambiguously different

Along the arrow of time, it flies
Unidirectional by design
Defying elegant symmetry
Sacrificing order to sublime

Resplendently calamitous
Silent agents of entropy
Conspiring to bring disorder
To our ordered philosophy

Many eons were spent evolving
Molding from the primordial clay
A nascent consciousness soon emerged
Seeking order from the disarray

Many minds began in earnest
To find meaning in the abstract
Unable to wrestle answers
From experience that they lacked

They set out to blindly discover
A new philosophy in the dark
Never knowing the complexity
Of this journey, they soon would embark

When witnessing cause and effect
They were unable to resolve
Why an egg can't be unscrambled
Another puzzle to be solved

While each spatial dimension affords
Movement along any direction
Time seems to resists this symmetry
In physics greatest insurrection

With time as the fourth dimension
Yet directions can be reversed
Why did agents of entropy
Prevent time from being traversed

Many evolved minds struggled greatly
Seeking a place among errant dust
Though determinism seemed to prevail
It was reality going bust

Deeper down the blackhole, they dove
Observational logic fails
Stubborn agents of entropy
Prevent elegance to avail

In arrogant juxtaposition
Convenient simplicity be damned
That wayward quantum of infinite
Defies all entropy out of hand

Crashing through the temporal gate
Arriving before it departs
This paradox of entropy
Brings it all right back to the start

The singularity burgeons
Agents of entropy now retire
Chaos coalesces to order
One last infinite quantum of fire

Earthbound Angel
Brandy Lane
from her book <u>Where Beautiful Loves</u>

Your smile dissolves
my dark and cold
landscape
into liquid
sunshine...
and flowers
bloom
in the depths
of my heart.

Brilliant colors
are everywhere
that gloomy grays
once covered.

Despair,
chaos
and hatred
give way to
peace,
hope
and love.

Calm,
beautiful
enunciation of words
that pour
from your lips,
are made thick
and deep
and beautiful
like honey
from the rarest
and most
exotic flowers.

The
sing-song
of your voice
lulls me into a trance
as you speak,
and takes me
into a place

that is safe,
where I am
cherished

and where the **Lord** knows
my name.

God
has given me
an earthbound angel
for a short time.
I cannot fathom
what I will do
when my time with you
comes to
an end.

Such a short time
to relish
in the presence
of your songs,
wrapped in your music,
bathed in your light.

I am comforted
in knowing that,
although we may have to part,
it isn't an eternal separation.

I will get to
play
and sing,
laugh
and smile,
and curl up
under your wings again someday.

And then,
I will praise
the Lord with you
for all eternity.

CAVAFY
John Grey

The wind blows out to sea
dry as thistles,
returns to me moist and dripping.
A gull circles, like a map-maker constantly
drawing the outline of the island
with its pearl-gray wings.
I love this feeling of shipwreck
and miracle intertwined.

Young men play cards, backgammon,
their wins, their losses,
slammed together,
no word that isn't a shout.
Others, half naked, cedar-skinned,
sprawl across pumice stone,
young dozing bulls in fields of sun.

I think of Cavafy,
a hundred years ago,
a man in shabby cinnamon suit
drinking in a working-class cafe,
admiring the latest Adonis crop,
statues of flesh that, were he a sculptor,
not a poet, he would carve into a likeness
he could love.

A young woman walks by me,
shy for all the earthiness of deep, dark eyes,
and full fleshy figure
on marble bones.
From skin to sea, the eye moves,
and the connection hovers
between lust and honesty.
She may be on the way
to market for all I know.
She may be tearful at
her father's small pension,
the pains in her stomach,
or hungry for a cigarette.

She is not part
of Cavafy's story.
In mine, however,
she's most welcome.

Mourning the Living
Jenna Zeihen

Dreams of snowflakes and clouds
In my mind's eye, those pieces of me never died
In whispers of *"what she could've been."*
I found myself becoming a *garden*,
Rather than a *bouquet*.
It's not what they thought I'd be
Lingering in rooms people thought I'd left
I hear words of condolences to the ones I love.
As if loving me is some great feat.
Some heartful act of charity.
As if my pure existence is something they feel liable to cry about
"Don't you wonder what she could've been?"
Like being a ghost, alive in a room
Hearing a more honest eulogy.

Seasonal Garden Visits
Debbie De Louise

Last year, I strolled through a garden
wrapped in autumn finery.
Burnished leaves of gold, crimson, and flame
blanketed my path in crunchy piles.
The sun kissed away the November shadows.

Billowy clouds whipped across a soft blue sky
like white sheets on a windswept clothesline.
Pine and evergreen scents perfumed the air.
Sparrows sang; squirrels scrambled
their songs and steps in time with fall.

I crossed a rustic bridge over a rambling brook
and followed a trail to the peaceful pond
where opalescent water lilies burst from their pads
and Chrysanthemums waved a greeting.

Winter came. I visited the garden again.
The trees were clad in white,
Their snowy branches, hanging low.
My boots trudged through the icy paths
a cold wind blew
the only sound around me
a silent echo

Spring found the garden in bloom
Tulips and daffodils raised their sleepy heads
It was time to wake from their lonely beds.

The scent of lilacs filled the air
Willows and cherry trees
shed their petals on the breeze
I spent time gazing over the lake
Where swans were floating in pairs.

Summer brought great bounty to the garden
Roses bloomed, filling trellises and bushes
Laughter floated from children
playing in the warm sun
Lovers lay on blankets, picnic baskets full
Days grew long but were soon done

Like plants, we follow the garden cycle of growing, aging,
death, and rebirth
As we live the autumns, winters,
springs, and summers,
of our seasons' life.

I'm not going... (Another lesson from Life)
Roy Duffield

I'm not going to tell you what you want to hear
                                  that you're special
                                       you look nice
                                  and there's nothing to fear.

I'm not going to apologise
but nor will you ever catch me
            telling you lies.

I'm not going to tell you
                        that you'll never remember this moment again
      for the rest of your years
and as long as you live
and for the rest of your life—
                                  this moment
         when you tried
to hold my hand
      but it wasn't mine.

I'm not coming
before you
in my Sunday best.
Instead here's my heart,
as seen
      through the scars
      on my chest.

I'm not silver-spoonfeeding you free,
bite-sized portions of sweetened, sugar-coated ready meals
                (and I scream!)
                and I'm not going to help you to keep it all down
           and I'm not going to be able to help you when you're down
                and I'm not going to turn any frowns upside down

I'm not going to be your dishwasher
                          your maid
I'm not going to build you a time machine
            or even a faster
             train.
I'm never going to help take away the pain
            nor reduce the irritation
            nor help you to sleep.

I'm not going to just sit here
            without so much as a peep.
    Show me your tears!
(and the milk
that you spilt
  on the passengers' seat)
  Show me your real tears!
and I'll show the real me.

I'm not going to give you what you want
                so dear,
go get it yourself
and when you do
I'll be the first one to cheer.

"Where I Find You"
A Nature-Inspired Poem of Remembrance
Shevaun Cavanaugh Kastl

"Where were you today!"

The words taste bitter as they fly from my mouth,
Pitched at the sky with the fury of the brittle, Winter wind.
I try to breathe, to fill my lungs with greedy gulps of frigid air
But the blood in my chest burns like Prairie Fire.
Grief is choking me, stealing my breath, as I struggle
To swallow a still-beating heart.

I collapse to the ground, forlorn and forsaken.
Exhaustion overtaking my over-wearied self…
Or the half that still remains, since you left.
Robbing me of a lifetime of unmade memories
and milestones you'll never be there for.
Now I'm fractured and broken and… I don't know where you are.

Angry tears spill from my eyes, staining my cheeks,
leaving salt-frosted rivulets in their wake.
I'm too vacant to care, too feeble to bother wiping them away,
So I watch them fall and pierce the ground
Like broken shards of glass.

A Church bell tolls. More splinters in my chest.
I cannot go back in that Chapel. But where else is there to go?

Take a walk with me.
The Voice is but a whisper, distant yet close.
It sounds like You, mellow and rich with a gentle, easy lilt.
Am I dreaming? Is this Delusion? Or could you, really be…
My heartbeat quickens. Temples pulsing, flutters fill my stomach,
And too long a moment passes of restrained but hopeful silence.

Somewhere behind me, the Chapel doors open,
But my heart rejects the intrusion.

Close your eyes. Follow my voice.
I still my breath, shutter my eyes…
and as the world before me disappears,
and the afterimage of my mind's eye recedes into the darkness
the cogs that move the wheel of time begin to turn. Back.

It's Summer in the Valley
Head to head on a carpet of wildflowers, we lay,
watching the clouds drifting above,
Spotting faces and places and mythical creatures.

I see a Unicorn. You see a giant Bear.
We swim in Lake Cole and build castles of sand,
I scaled the rock wall. Your hand always guiding me.

Late Summer evenings of stargazing.
You read the night sky. I listen, enraptured
To celestial bedtime stories authored by flickering constellations.
Every blink, every wink holds a secret, you say.
I smile and you laugh.
Motion capture.

I open my eyes, flushed with nostalgia
Surprised to find myself standing at the bridge.
The water below is a sheet of ice.
The slabs of wood slick with freezing rain.
I should turn back, but I don't. I close my eyes
And You're back with me again.

It's Autumn in the Valley.
The air is crisp and fragrant, sweet and sour and smokey
Like dew-kissed leaves and harvest apples and charred wood.
Bundled in the warmth of your green, cable knit sweater,
My hand is in yours, though I don't have need for it.
"Go ahead Shevaun. You're fine on your own. I'll be right behind you."
And you always were.

I'm walking through the Woods.
Following the Echos of Voices from the past,
Our Voices. Laughing and chanting in tandem…
"Once you reach the giving tree, count your steps to number three
pivot left to find the quarry and the relics of our story."
This is the way to the Time Capsule.

Through the maze of tangled roots and trailing vines
I see the specters of Us. Fencing with lances of sunshine
piercing the crimson-gold canopy of leaves overhead.
Spinning in pools of Amber-lucent Autumn light
As falling leaves flutter and twirl around us.
The Valley was our Fantasia

I've reached the Quarry. Though I remember It being bigger.
I close my eyes once again.

It's Winter in the Valley
The giant trees are bending,

Their boughs weighed down with snow, creating doors to Narnia
My 22 year old self adds an arrowhead to the box.
And another rock to the pile.
And then I turn and time slows down
Your picture comes in frame.

It was our last trip to the Valley.
You were still well. You were still smiling. You were still…
Here. I'm here.

My fingers are soiled and clutching the tin box
tight to my chest which is heaving and heavy.
Unwelcome reality. I want to go back.
Or I want to go forward.
Squeezing eyes-wide-shut,
And begging the memories to come.

What of the Spring? What of Dandelion dreams?
Countless wishes blown in the wind…
What of Butterfly wings and butterfly kisses?
Crown wreathes of flowers? And paper boat races down the creek…

That is where you find me.

All at once I feel the kiss of snow upon my cheek.
Downy soft like the change of light, now hazy in hues
Of lavender and gold. Fat flakes of snow drift down around me,
Quelling all sound in a reverent, holy hush…
And then you speak again.

There is heaven above and heaven below
And both are of our own making.
Do not dwell in me, remember me…
When the seasons change and the sun rises and sets,
Remember me. But only a little.
Then bottle me up, put me back in the drawer,
And live your life as I taught you…

"*Love with abandon, fall with Grace and find hope everywhere.*"
As I step from the podium, my words echo back to me. Your words.
They're all I hear as I walk down the aisle,
Still broken-hearted, but no longer shackled with despair.
The sunrise brings a new day… and another walk through time with you.
And so I dare to hope again, for I know now where I find you.

Russian Standard
Marina Antropow Cramer

1

We raise paper cups to our lips
Our throats receive imported firewater
It burns good, this bitter communion
Loosens our tongues.

Behind us the backhoe grinds,
Lifts red earth by the bucketful until we can no longer hear the thud of dirt on our mother's casket.
No, it's not disrespectful, this orange machinery.
Who uses shovels anymore?
A day's work for the living, she would have said. The dead don't mind.

2

Sifting through recollections, I am a child here at the cemetery,
Conjuring the phantom of old Varvara open for business,
Her Chevy station wagon parked over there, near the lending library where my mother often left stacks of last year's mimeographed newsletters outside the door.
A donation, she said. They'll know what to do with them.

Immigrants throw nothing away.

Old Varvara nods, too busy for small talk.
Her white kerchief, worn the peasant way above the eyebrows, double tied under the chin.
The abacus zings and clacks under her swift fingers.
A day's work, a livelihood.
My young mother buys smoked sprats, honey, freshly fermented sauerkraut.
Kvass, homemade, in corked milk bottles, to drink with Sunday dinner.
Candy from the old country – *Mishka, Korovka, Lastochka.*

I will find the wrappers pressed smooth, in a greeting card box next to her bed, among passport photographs, a key, a tiny doll in crocheted dress and cap.

3

We miss the potato salad, *pelmeni*, perfect meat pie.
The way she listened for signs of discord: Make peace with one another. Now.
And we obeyed.

Excerpt from Whisper Dancing
J Hirtle

November 9, 1918- East Boston

"Jimmy, I have something for you." In her hand, she held a toy wooden top. A dull gray string wound tightly around the bell-shaped middle.

"It was Dad's when he was a boy. I found it in the footlocker, beneath all the old sweaters he would never throw out."

Jimmy held the toy in his hand. It was a toy for little boys. Rubbing his thumb over the string, it was smooth against his skin, well worn. He thought of his father. Once upon a time he had been a young boy playing with this toy. We struggle to imagine our parents as being children. Most often we have little desire to imagine them as any less than who they are and have always been. For Jimmy Quinn it was easier thinking of his father as forever gone.

The boy pushes away the thoughts and puts the wooden top in the pocket of his robe. His mother kisses him on the cheek, "I will see you tomorrow, Jimmy. God willing."

From the window seat, Jimmy watched his mother and sister move hurriedly down the street. Their heads tucked down, seeking protection from the frigid wind. Back in his room, young Mr. Quinn lay on the mattress, holding the wooden top in his hand, crestfallen his mother had not asked him if he wanted to go out with them.

You didn't ask her, Jimmy Quinn.

He stares at the toy as if the phantom voice belonged to it.

"And she didn't offer," he informs the wooden toy.

Sitting up, he expands the noose, and he slips the string over his finger. His hand remembers playing with a toy top when he was eight- or nine-years young. A time when pandemic was a word he did not know. The days before an invisible enemy placed a leprous mahogany kiss upon the cheeks of its victims. A time when his father tucked him into bed at night with a reminder to ask God to wake him come morning.

If I should die before I wake...

Palming the toy, he places his thumb across the flat top. He flicks his wrist. The toy bangs against the hard floor before tumbling on its side like a drunken sailor. Jimmy retrieves the toy, wraps the worn string around the bulbous body and flings it again, neglecting to secure the string to his finger. The toy flies across the room like a loosed canary and crashes into the oak wardrobe; the string unwound and glaring accusingly at the boy. He stares at his hand in disbelief before again retrieving the toy top, winding the string, carefully placing the miniature noose over his finger. He cocks his wrist, takes aim, and lets loose. The spinning toy lands on the metal nub spinning so fast the colors blur into one magical hue. With the delight of a young boy, Jimmy Quinn watches the toy dance and spin across the floor, hopping over cracked varnish without fear of losing balance. A fine toy it was to bring delight to this lad amid melancholy.

The top wobbles as the spinning slows. It turns across the floor, spins once more, falls on its side before rolling under the aged wardrobe. The boy crawls quickly across the floor, the long string dangling from his finger following like an obedient dog. Peering under the monstrous hunk of furniture, Jimmy spies the toy lying on its side atop layers of dust. Blindly, he stretches his lean arm under the wardrobe, searching for the toy. Dust covers his hand and sleeve as he repositions to try again. With his second and third failed attempts, Jimmy Quinn sits with his back against the oak armoire wondering why he was trying so hard to reach a toy that moments ago he had thought as a childish dreck. *Nothing else to do,* he told himself. The boy looks around the room for something to stretch his reach. His bat! *That will do the trick!* Laying on his side, he peeks under the furniture searching for the toy. He closes one eye. It didn't help but seemed like the thing to do. Rolling the bat over the dust-covered floor, he listens for the sound of the bat hitting the wooden top. Peering

again into the darkness beneath the wardrobe, further back. He pushes that bat. *Clunk*. Jimmy freezes at the deliverance of the hollow sound. The only muscle moving was a twitch over his left eye. His momma told him the twitch came when he was thinking too hard on something.
What was that? He pushes the bat forwarded again (having now forgotten about the toy). *Clunk, clunk.*

The oak wardrobe is heavy. With his shoulder against it and three deep grunts, he manages to move the wardrobe away from the wall. Instead of the wall of plaster and fading paint, he had expected to see, there is a door. His eyes adjust as the light breaks through the shadows long held behind by the armoire. The door is heavy, not like the paper-thin door to his bedroom. Four rectangular panels decorate the door's face. A handle of carved crystal reflects the unexpected light. A dark brass template shaped like an hourglass reveals the keyhole. *A skeleton key.* The miniscule muscle above his eye twitches. Grabbing the knob, he turns it clockwise. No. Counterclockwise. Nothing. Dropping to one knee, Jimmy inspects the keyhole. He can see light coming from the other side of the door. Moving closer, he places his eye against the opening.

His grandfather had told him of the changes made to the apartments when the immigrant population had exploded. *We had the space of a king's castle;* he had told Jimmy as he slipped the sharp blade of his pocketknife across the soapstone. *But the greedy capitalist respect no one. They tore down one wall to put up two. They blocked the doors to our bedroom and stole our keys. A king couldn't turn around to piss in this place now.*

On the other side of the door, through the keyhole, is a large room. Twice as large as his own. He sees a window draped with sheer linen. To the right of the window, hanging on the wall, is a portrait surrounded by a dark frame. The painting is of a man and a woman. A small child sits upon the woman's lap. The man wore the uniform of an officer. He was tall, with dark eyes and square-chinned. They look like a happy family, Jimmy thought. Beneath the painting is a long narrow table. A rectangular brown box with six black knobs and one large silver knob sat on the end of the table. Jimmy had never seen a radio but had heard his father talk about them. Next to the box (radio?) was another brown box. Slighter and polished to a high shine. Jimmy read the script written across the top, *Edison*. A music machine! They must be rich, he thought.

A flash of blue crosses in front of his eyes. Pulling back from the door, he almost loses his balance. His voyeuristic adventure rains remorse down upon the boy fearful he had been caught peeking through the keyhole. He struggles to still his breathing, believing it to be louder than it was. Sitting with his back against the door, his heart thumping against his breast, he musters the courage to return to his covert vantage point.

The first time he saw her, she was standing in the middle of the room. She wore a long blue flowing dress, the color of the spring sky. The sleeves were too long, reaching to the base of her willowy fingers. Her arms down, crossed at the wrists and resting in front of her. The collar was high on her neck in the fashion of royalty. Long auburn hair cascaded over slender shoulders, framing the most beautiful face this young man had ever beheld. Her eyes are closed. Her nose is narrow and slopes gracefully. Her mouth set firm. Her lips soft, red like a strawberry picked from a farmer's field. And then a faint smile. What did she see behind closed eyes to bring a smile to her lips? Jimmy presses his cheek against the brass plate, hoping to see more.

Slowly the girl raises her arms above her head. Her wrists remain crossed as if knotted by an invisible cord. Her chest rises as she inhales deeply. Her smile falters, lips held together tightly. Jimmy Quinn watches with amazement as the girl seems to grow taller. Unseen, beneath the long blue dress, the girl arches her feet clad with satin point shoes, creating the illusion witnessed by the eyes on the other side of the keyhole.

She knows he is watching.

A Dream Paralysis
Sejo Jose

Project Maya

She was very upset with her husband and her mother. Enough is enough, she thought. "I have failed in life. And he and mom do not understand it. Maybe dad was courageous in doing something about it." She still remembered seeing her dad's lifeless body on the bed, overdosed on sleeping pills with a smile on the face.

She had been pondering over the email she received over a month back – it sought participation for a 6-month project by a private armed forces company. It was either this or suicide on her mind. She decided to go for it. She wrote a letter to her mom and husband that she was taking a break and they will not be seeing her for some time. "I love you," she concluded.

She called the number provided and went to the location. She is told it is a sleep experiment to study the impact of sleep on memories. She signed the 5-page form barely reading through the details in small fonts. The place is calming, she thought to herself. The place was indeed well-designed with proper lighting to make participants comfortable.

During dinner, they were told that the project – Project Maya – would start the next day. Most participants were patients with a history of depression and attempted suicides. The main doctor congratulated them for being part of the project.

The next morning, all of them were asked to wear a reddish military uniform. They were asked to enter a small cabin and lie down. They were given injections that put them to sleep. Within 10 minutes, every participant was asleep.

A new dawn

Everyone woke up the next day. They got a healthy breakfast, and some cash. They were happy, with no depressive or suicidal thoughts. They felt their life had a purpose. Everyone went back to their homes, looking forward to meeting their people.

She was happy to see her husband and her mother again. She said she would not want to leave them for anything in the world. She re-joined her workplace and started enjoying her work. Days passed by fast, and she was loving every bit of it. After five months, she started thinking – "how come my life is so perfect?" The thought kept nagging her to the point that it was the only thing that she could think of.

She spoke to her husband about it and he said that it is because of her improved mindset towards life. He said she had effectively stopped getting fixated on negative aspects of life and had accepted life for what it is. She was happy to hear that. She was thankful that she had not given up on life like her father.

After a few days, the thought came back – "how come my life is so perfect?" She avoided the question but gave in after a while and started to look at ways to finds out why everything is so good in her life. She suddenly woke up with a jerk and started panting.

What happened to my hair?

Her eyes were wide with curiosity at what she saw. There were several people in transparent sleeping pods, with monitoring electrodes attached to their bald heads, inside a large white hall. She could only see that much and tried to get out of her own pod, but something held her neck back. The narrow pod's design barred her from turning her spine enough to see anything other than a blue cable, which was seemingly connected to the back of her neck. She felt her own head, and thought "What happened to my hair?" She tried to pull herself up but her neck ached as she did.

"Maybe I can help with that" a baritone voice from somewhere said. She saw the project doctor walking inside the hall. He came and unclipped the cable from the back of her head. He helped her to come out of her pod. "Can I take you for a walk around?" he asked politely.

The place seemed strange to her as she walked around with the doctor. A large hall that was painted in white all around with air-conditioned vents on the ceiling. She recognized some of the faces in the sleeping pods from the day she joined the project. Everyone was wearing the same red military uniform. The doctor was observing her body language and facial expressions. She was speechless as she tried to make sense of what is happening.

The nice doctor speaks

The doctor told her not to panic. "They are sleeping peacefully. Since you are the first one of them to wake up, it is my duty to help you make sense of it," he said, and waited to see how she reacted. When he saw that she was listening quietly, he continued.

"Our project was designed to make the perfect soldiers, the perfect machines to carry out difficult operations in the world. Our scientists designed a way to keep people in a sleep mode where they dream, of a perfect life. We could tap their insecurities and give them the perfect solutions so that everything happened as they wanted them to." The doctor waited for her response, which did not come, and so he continued.

"Meanwhile, when they are awake they are in a hypnotized state. Just before we wake them up, we use a difficult brainwashing procedure for their sub-conscious mind so that they are ready to carry out orders. Once they are ready after a 20-minute briefing, they carry out our orders with accuracy. Perfect to the tee, you see. Any operation, anywhere. The perfect soldiers. I see you have some questions."

"Yes," she said. "These people believe their dreams to be their real life. Am I correct?"

"Very much miss."

"But what about their memories from these operations? And what is people recognize them?"

"Well, once the job is done, we recall them and put them to sleep, during which we effectively erase their memories. And they wear masks during operations so no one would recognize them. The perfect soldiers."

"What are these operations?"

"They are various – we have only undertaken 3 so far, with 3 separate sets of soldiers. One operation was to exfiltrate some government documents for a client. Another involved adding some ingredients in a snack manufacturer's raw materials. The third involved robbing an embassy. But you need not worry. You have not had your first operation yet."

"I do not understand. How is this allowed? These people are being kept without their will. Is the law not doing anything? And why was I targeted? Why did you send me the emails? What if I do not want to be part of the project anymore? What about my hair?"

"That is a lot of questions dear miss. We are not keeping them without their consent. They signed the consent form themselves. It's a pity none of you read it, but that was expected. We are a private company that provide private services, and not entirely under the purview of the law. As to why we chose you and others like you, well, our analytics tools showed us that all of you were suicidal and were desperate for a getaway. Data does not lie you see. Your data behaviour also showed us that all of you are lazy enough to not read documents before signing, which is why we knew none of you would read the devil in the details. We shaved everyone's hair for uniformity. You cannot leave, but I can offer you a different role with us. We can discuss that after dinner of course," he said in a tone that was commanding, but restrained.

"Why have I woken up, and not these others?"

"There are glitches in any procedure. You were the only one who questioned things, and that is why you were the only one who woke up. That's the first time we had a glitch like that. Come now, dinner is here."

After dinner, she was told that her new role will start the next day, and then she was compelled to lie on the bed. She dozed off in some time. But she soon woke up and escaped the premises through the window. She ran to a nearby motel. She told the motel owner that said she needed to go home in a car, and that she will pay once she reached home.

On the way, she kept praying that her mom and husband are alive. She reached home and hugged her husband as soon as he opened the door. Both of them started crying out of joy, joined by her mother, in an embrace. She seemed to understand true happiness as she paid and thanked the motel owner. That night was the happiest in her life. She cried to sleep in her husband's arms, thankful to God for everything.

"Project report, doctor"

The doctor spoke to her sleeping body inside the pod. "I gave you happiness and everything else you wished for. I gave you a perfect life. Why would anyone question that? You are indeed special. I am really sad to let you die." He walked to the floor above with an explanation for his superior.

"Project report, doctor" the lady said in a questioning tone, as she smiled, bending her head slightly down to see the doctor beyond her reading glasses. "I would need that in writing as well," she continued with the same smile.

"Well," the doctor said, "the subject, in her dream mode, questioned the perfection of her life, and woke out of the dream. I told her the truth about us. But as you always say, we can't have any loose ends, and so we are putting her into a permanent sleep. Once I explained to her about us, I fed her the special dinner, and put her to sleep. Once she dozed off, we took her to the sleeping pod and reinitiated the dream sequence. I made her dream about escaping from us, meeting her family and sleeping in her husband's arms. Since, in her dreams, she is sleeping, we expect her to die without any dream back-feeding malfunction in the system. I have ensured that she does not dream within the dream. We'll close her in 5 minutes."

The superior seemed satisfied. "You did well doctor. With so many cases of missing people in the news, we can't afford to have any loose ends," she said.

"Thank you very much. And good night ma'am," the doctor said, as he saw her waving goodbye to him.

He went down and turned the switch off. As he watched her pulse confirm her death, he was amused to see that she had been smiling. "I am glad you died with a smile on your face. A lifeless body with a smile on the face. Now all I have to do is convince my conscience that at least you were happy when you died. God bless your soul, my dear."

Melissa and the Stone Troll
Elana Gomel

Once there was a little girl who loved to eat. She ate bread and butter; ham and eggs; cherries and apricots. She particularly liked honey-cake, and so her parents named her Melissa, which means "honey".

Famine came to her village, and her parents died. Melissa survived but she became gaunt and pinched. She wandered into the dark forest where she met a stone troll.

"Little girl, why are you sad?" he asked.

"I am hungry!"

"Don't your parents feed you well?"

Only then did Melissa remember that her parents were dead.

"Look at me," said the troll. "I never want for sustenance; and I never grow wrinkled and sad. We are what we eat. I eat rock, and rock is eternal."

Indeed, the troll's face was as white as alabaster and his eyes as blue as sapphires. Poor Melissa thought she had never seen anyone so beautiful.

"Tell you what," said the troll. "I'll trade with you. I'll take your hunger and I'll give you my satiety. You'll never lack food again."

"But I don't want to eat rock!" said Melissa. "They'll break my teeth!"

"You can eat ashes and coals," the troll said. "They'll make you as bright and lively as fire."

Melissa who was too hungry to remember that one should not trade with trolls, agreed. The troll took her human appetite and immediately metamorphosed into a handsome young man. He walked happily away, only pausing to throw over his shoulder:

"Oh, I forgot to tell you. There is one catch. You can eat coal and ashes, you can even swallow flame, and it'll keep you alive. But human food will be poison to you."

Melissa wandered in the forest for many days until she came to king's palace. There she was hired as a kitchen wench. This suited her just fine because she could rake ashes, clean fireplaces, and collect coals. She swallowed fire and it made her eyes bright, her hair red, and her temper volatile. But she still missed human food. So she confronted the chef and made him teach her everything he knew about cooking. In a short while, she forced him to resign – like everybody else, the chef was afraid of this fiery girl with her unpredictable flares of anger.

So Melissa, who now called herself Cinderella because she ate cinders, became the cook. She cooked wonderful dishes, far more elaborate than the old chef's best creations. But she could never taste her own food; she could only remember the country fare lovingly prepared for her by her parents. And often her tears fell into the pot she was stirring, adding an additional flavor to it.

The king, pleased with the improvement of his table, wished to meet the new cook. And when Melissa appeared, he was instantly smitten with her sparkling beauty and proposed marriage to her. Melissa looked at the young king and for the first time since her parents' death felt a hunger for another person's company. For fire only consumes itself, while food is made to be shared with others.

But the king's evil councilor remonstrated and told the king those wonderful dishes were surely a slow poison. For how else to explain that the girl never tasted her own creations?

Melissa saw the doubt in the king's eyes. She took a slice of her marvelous honey cake and put it into her mouth.

And the trade with the troll was undone. She became, once again, a country girl, sweet as honey and soft as butter. But the king who wanted a spirited, impetuous wife decided not to marry her after all.

HEAD COUNT
Joe Baumann

To prove a point to my husband, I call up all of my ex-boyfriends and ask them to come over.

"Sure," they say. "Be there soon."

They arrive over the course of two days, some flying from faraway places like Minsk or Budapest, others driving in. They bring gifts: wine or plants, succulents we can keep and poinsettias we can't because of the cats. My husband watches them traipse through the house from the couch. He refuses to answer the door if I'm leading one of them to the backyard when another bashes the bell.

"This is ridiculous, Peter," he says when the twentieth ex-boyfriend arrives.

"You wanted to know."

"Not this badly."

"Okay everyone," I say when they're all milling about in our yard. It's spacious, angular, lush with St. Augustine grass. The ex-boyfriends watch me and wait for further instructions. I tell them we're going to make a giant abacus. As soon as I say so, they're lining up as if they all know what shape they should make, and they do. I rush back inside for the hank of white yarn I bought store after I made the phone calls.

"Okay," my husband says. "I get it."

"We're not finished yet," I say. "I don't think I've proved myself to you quite yet."

"Yes, you have," he says. He's standing at our kitchen island, a glass of white wine in front of him. He never drinks when the sun is up unless he's golfing. It's why he's lean and fit. "Please, Peter."

"We're almost there," I say. "Hold tight."

Outside, I shear off long swaths of the yarn and loop one around each ex's waist.

"Now let's count," I say. "Oh, but wait." I call for my husband. The ex-boyfriends stare at him with a combination of jealousy and dismissal. He doesn't come out, so I yell louder. I can feel blood in my throat. Finally, he slides the door open and steps onto the patio. His wineglass is nearly empty. His eyes are squinted.

"You see?" I say.

"I do." He rubs his face. "You've been in plenty of relationships."

"Exactly."

"We done now?"

"Do you not want to know how many?"

"I've been counting as they arrived."

"So then you know."

"I do."

"Great."

"Yes."

I turn to my ex-boyfriends and wave at them. "You guys can go now. Thanks for coming."

They offer *you're welcomes* and *are you sures* and when I flutter my fingers they start dispersing into clumps like this is a garden party. I ignore them. I sigh and lean into my husband's chest. He grasps me around the shoulders, careful not to lose the last of his wine. We go inside, where I pour myself a glass, empty the bottle topping him off. We stand there and drink, watching my ex-boyfriends mill about, unsure of themselves. I rub my husband's arm. Soon, we'll probably make out, make love, and argue about something else, a fight I'm sure to win.

Dreams Are the Opposite to Reality
A.O. Wallat

The man minded the gap and stepped onto the train. He sat down and placed his bag beside him. The doors bleeped, hissed, then slid closed and the train left the station.

The journey was bumpy. The carriage rocked from side to side and the man, wary of his luggage, held the bag in place to keep it from falling. Soon the train stopped at another station and the carriage filled up and the man had to move his bag for another passenger.

Then he had a problem. The bag was too large to rest on his lap and if he laid it between his legs other passengers wouldn't be able to get passed. So he opted to place it by the sliding doors. This made him nervous.

What if someone snatches it? He asked. I would have to chase them down, he answered. But what if I was too slow? He wondered. Well, just make sure you don't lose it. He agreed.

So he chose to watch his bag the whole time. But the journey was long. And soon his eyelids began to close. He had to keep watch but couldn't. Instead, he made a compromise. Between stops he would sleep. No, rest his eyes. And at every stop he would watch his bag. And so he did.

The bag was there. The doors bleeped and hissed. He shut his eyes. The doors bleeped and hissed. He opened his eyes. The bag was still there. The doors hissed. He shut his eyes. He opened his eyes. The carriage was empty. The bag was not there. The train leapt off the tracks. It flew. Then he was flying. The doors bleeped and hissed. He opened his eyes. The bag was there again. He waited for the hiss and then closed his eyes once more. He was outside. Running. Running after the train. It stopped. The doors hissed. He got on. The bag was still there. The doors bleeped. He opened his eyes.

It was his stop. The doors were sliding shut. He jumped up. And got out just in time. He closed his eyes. The bag was still there.

Sanctuary
Benedetto Varotta

When she approached him he was wary. He never trusted people in business suits. Especially not these government kooks. But this woman approached him with clicking heels and asked if she could pet his dog. Her voice was hoarse and smooth like cracked sugar. The dog, always happy to receive pets and belly rubs, wagged its tail and sniffed her hand, inspecting it for food.

"What's your name?" she asked as she knelt down, ID badge dangling from her neck. He did not want to speak, at first.

"Frank," he said.

"How sweet. I love dogs with human names." Frank looked down, slightly embarrassed.

"Oh," he said, "My name is Frank. That's Maxie." She chuckled and pet Maxie's head, standing back up and pulling out a tablet,

"Well, both are nice names," she said. "It's nice to meet you, Frank. My name is Linda Cosgrove." She did not extend her hand but instead started tapping on the screen as she spoke, her eyes behind her glasses darting around the screen. "Are you familiar with the HFH?"

He shook his head. Partly because he did not really know, and partly because he wanted her to leave. Frank hoped that his disinterest would sway her to leave, but she continued talking.

A few years ago, when the world went sick, Frank lost his job and never recovered. Nobody needed him. The world surpassed the need for taxi drivers. They were obsolete. People stopped going places and when they started again the apps took over. People wanted to ride in clean cars, not filthy taxis. When rent was due it stayed that way until he was evicted. There was no government compensation, his parents were dead and he lived alone. There was no help.

30 million people lost their homes. 30 million people to the streets across the country, sectioned off into packed alleyways and barred off parts of town, living in squalor. Most died from illness, but those who survived could barely call this a life.

People seldom gave him money. They'd ask if he was going to use it for drugs. Even when he told them No, and shakily pressed his hands together as if in prayer, they'd sprinkle out some change. Though because of the national coin shortage they became more valuable, so people held onto their pennies as if they were crystals. Some restaurants offered free food in exchange for coins, as if the words Free and Exchange could coexist.

He'd spend his days listening to the cars drive by, the aggravating honking and cursing. The hiss of steam from cracked sidewalks and construction. New buildings were erected around the city over the past year. Government-type refuges. Homes for the Homeless, they were called. Because the city was to be clean.

Since these sanctuaries, they were called, were built, homelessness was at an all time low. Slowly these sections became less congested. People were being recruited to live in these government homes. Frank could never imagine himself ever being chosen, and wondered what he would do he was offered the opportunity to sleep in a bed again. That opportunity arose with Linda Cosgrove.

"Come stay with us!" she said after delivering her speech. Her smile was crooked.

Frank, still skeptical of this woman, accepted her offer. What else was there for him to lose in this world?

"I'm bringing my dog," he said.

"Yes, of course," Linda said. "We'll have you fill out a small amount of paperwork and assign you to a room. We'll have a nice warm meal for you waiting at the unit." She tapped some more on the tablet and he followed her down the street.

The building was not tall but the outside was mirrored and Frank observed himself in the reflection. He couldn't remember the last time he really looked at himself. He was old, he noticed, forgetful of his age. His hair was greying but not white but the grease turned it dark. It lay straggled at his shoulders. He noticed his skin covered in grime, the dark reflection painting spots on his neck and cheeks. A beard with similar texture to Maxie splayed itself across his chin down to his Adam's apple. Glancing at his fingers, they were skinny and dark with dirt under his long nails. His appearance made him sad, something similar to shame, but Linda spoke, putting a hand on his back where she could feel the point of his shoulder blades.

"It's alright, Frank," she said. "We'll take care of you here."

And he believed her. Because what else was there to believe in besides God and a reckoning?

She put her wrist up to a scanner of some sort and the two doors slid open with a whine. He followed her inside. The interior was unexpected. Empty, but colorful, plastered with light pinks and blues that reminded Frank of bubblegum, though the room smelled of citrus cleaning products and varnish that burned the hairs in his nose. There were stations with tablets to answer survey questions, he presumed, but Linda motioned forward past them. "You'll get a chance to fill those out later," she said. "First, let's get you cleaned up."

When they walked farther down the hallway, soft music played over speakers somewhere but it was covered in a film of static—this low hum that distorted the sound, reminding Frank of something demonic. Maxie followed beside him until they reached two large metal doors. Two men stood on either side of the entrance dressed in what seemed to be boiler suits, dark navy and steam-pressed.

Frank began to feel uneasy. Perhaps it was something to do with the possibility of a new life. The newness of a sanctuary, some haven to call home even if only for a moment. He would let himself deserve this, he thought. He imagined a bath, not a shower, because he missed taking baths, the ascension in water. The scent of urine leaving his skin. A haircut and a bowl of stew that he would share with Maxie. He breathed out and looked around while Linda scanned her wrist again.

Frank noticed chipped tiles and melting paint on the walls. The smell of something musty now as he got closer to the doors. He wondered if it was just him. The doors cranked open revealing a small room, dark metal and uninviting. There was another set of doors identical to those that just opened on the other side.

"Your new home is just on the other side of those doors," Linda said. Maxie whimpered and shook beside Frank. He pet him and whispered that it would be okay, even if he did not believe it himself. "Go on ahead, we'll take Maxie with us to the grooming chamber so he can get cleaned up, too." She smiled that awkward, crooked smile at him and took Maxie by the collar.

"I don't want to leave him," Frank said.

"It's alright, Frank. He will be in good hands," Linda said.

"What is this?"

"I'm sorry, Frank, it's what's best."

Frank tried to insist but when he grabbed for Maxie, the two men took him by the arms, his thin bones, and thrust him into the room. He fell to his knees with a bang. The doors shut behind him and he tried to scream but no sound came out. If he wasn't so old, so weak, maybe he could have done something, he thought. But there was a groan of gears and the room began to descend. The static music droned as the shaft scraped against the walls on its way down. Soon, it became the only thing Frank could hear. Even the whimpering dog fell silent, and the sounds of the city so far above him now.

The Cowboy
Evren Kadir Sezgin

I am a cowboy. And while I told this to no one, I discussed what it meant to be one with Dr. Everett Nicholson. He asked me what it was that cowboys did. The doctor had large hands that folded over the notepad he scribbled on. His body folded in so many ways. His chest doubled over his legs as he balanced his papers on his thighs. His face sagged and his chin collapsed into his neck. I began to look for another fold in Dr. Everett Nicholson when he sighed and rose to his feet. I was certain the skin on his right ankle creased over the top of his foot, and I looked to see if they had when the doctor snapped his fingers in front of my face, beaconing my attention.

He asked me again what it was that cowboys did. In the darkness of his shadow that loomed over me, I said cowboys were defined by what they were able to save. Dr. Everett Nicholson corrected me, and said I meant whom. *Who* they were able to save. He was right. His shadow receded to the chair he sat in moments before, and asked his next question.

Outside, Toronto taunted me and I decided not to hear the doctor the first time he spoke. The Don Valley Parkway sprouts with colour, greens and blues burned my eyes. Potted lilies that Dr. Everett Nicholson tended to in between appointments, stood in the wind, and swallowed yellow honey bees whole. A venus flytrap neighbored the flowers, and they too swallowed the bees all at once. I wondered which plant, if the chance ever arose, I would cut first.

Dr. Everett Nicholson stomped his foot, his knee folded over his shoe, and asked his question again. Had I earned the title of cowboy?

From the main street outside his office, I threw rocks at the doctor's potted plants. Dr. Everett Nicholson was right, I had yet to save anyone from anything, and yet I wanted to hurt him as he had hurt me. A cement block broken up by time was heavy in my hands and I was unable to swing it high enough to reach the doctor's office on the second floor of his clinic.

At the crosswalk that cut through Spadina Ave. and King St., I carved *fuck dr. EN* on the trunk of a maple tree and, pieces of bark in my hand, realized how easily I am able to destroy things. The stars began to show themselves in the summer night as I exited the pharmacy, pills prescribed by Dr. Everett Nicholson in one hand, the bark of the maple tree still in the other.

A clean stroller, plastic tarp purposefully placed over its carriage, rolled into the wall of the pharmacy, abandoned on the sidewalk. I turned, noticing I was the only stranger to stand as witness of this, and looked at the contents of both my hands. They were full, and I made the decision to save no one and cross the corner of King St. and Spadina Ave. without checking to see if the stroller was inhabited.

I returned to an empty apartment and threw the bark I'd held onto in the garbage. Five minutes later, I stood at the pharmacy's wall, only to find the stroller ravaged. Its carriage was missing and its plastic tarp torn to shreds. Littered on the ground was what I could only presume to be the belongings of whatever lived inside of it, a pink baby blanket and broken pocket mirror discarded in the street's nearest flood drain.

Summer turns to fall and fall turns to winter and both Toronto and I become unbearable. I saw the stroller everywhere. In the snow that piled on my balcony, and overcame the two chairs and table set to overlook the city's skyline. In the bathroom mirror when I exited the shower and called my naked reflection a cowboy. In the barren trees of the Don Valley Parkway and the withered lilies sat between hills of snow that cluttered Dr. Everett Nicholson's balcony.

While I only returned to the same pharmacy a month after last seeing the stroller to refill my prescription, I was unable, despite my best efforts, to not look towards the wall where the stroller sat. Now empty, stained with what I could only assume was dog piss, I dug my feet in the bank of snow that flooded the sidewalks gutter, and cursed aloud.

I said this no one, though a passing stranger walking their dog turned towards me, and I believed they hoped I was talking to them.

I returned to my apartment only to be welcomed by the frustration of winter. The latch of the sliding door that separated my living room and balcony was broken, and snow carpeted the apartment's hardwood flooring. And this too, reminded me of the stroller.

I only remembered February was part of winter when the first of the month arrived and the snow had yet to dissipate. By this time, I had only returned to the empty wall next to the pharmacy to refill the pills Dr. Everett Nicholson promised would help me, and still the empty wall haunted me.

As if to spite winter, the stroller only returned to the corner of Spadina Ave. and King St. in the spring. Outside of the pharmacy, a bag of white pills in my hand, I stared it down. I was certain, in that moment, I was a lone cowboy, eyeing the scoundrel that threatened my title. I threw the pills to the ground, forgetting there was no snow to catch them, and took the carriage of the stroller with both hands.

This was it. This was when I proved to Dr. Everett Nicholson that he was wrong. I was a cowboy.

The dry skin on my hands had yet to defrost from the winter months, and splintered red lines formed on my knuckles as I pressed against the stroller's black fabric.

I cursed aloud, though no one was on the street to hear it.

The carriage's plastic tarp was so heavy when I tried to tear it off. I screamed and screamed until it tore in half. I looked into the stroller, finally able to save whomever it was I abandoned last summer.

Inside, tucked under a lavender blanket, a pocket mirror reflected the image of not a cowboy, but just - me. I threw the carriage into the alley hidden between the pharmacy and its neighbor, and stepped back into the empty sidewalk.

Now, the stroller was, as I had found it back in the summer, ravaged. Its carriage was missing and its plastic tarp torn to shreds. The carriage was, of course, missing because I threw it, and the plastic, well…

Littered on the ground was the lavender blanket and mirror, now broken, the contents emptied hazardly onto the sidewalk when I threw the carriage.

From around the corner, a man buttoned into a brown shirt and cow print vest walked by me and stepped his oversized black boots over the wrecked stroller in front of him. He took a moment to pause afterward and looked back at me. He said *they* got him too, and before he vanished turning around the next block, he called me a cowboy.

ZERO
Leigh Alder

On a day like any other, I wouldn't linger; I'd stop in several rooms to make notes and stroll around outdoors to observe and move on. But this wasn't a day like any other. I'd watched her struggle across the parking lot with the taste of greasy nickels in her mouth, sucking in against the steel bands stiffening the back of her neck. So, I followed her into the classroom in the shabby trailer and slid to the back corner and had a seat on top of a built-in bookshelf that had seen better decades. I smiled, an expression that most people don't understand.

The children came and went. They were teenagers and wouldn't like being called children, but every adult knows that's what they still are. They were noisy entering, but they settled. They took out their notebooks and papers and pens, and they learned. Even the ones who didn't really want to. But, I wasn't there to see them; I came for their teacher. A vibrant fifty-something and popular with the kids. They liked her because she was smart and funny and knew how to teach. They trusted her; she watched over them and cheered them on.

I know she saw me; I could see the sweat, glazing her forehead, moistening her upper lip. But she tried to ignore me, tried to pretend I hadn't come. She carried on as best she could.

During classes on a day like any other, she moved around the room from desk to desk, learner to learner, answering questions and making suggestions. She usually didn't sit during class at all. I remember she sat that day.

One class had rolled in and then rolled out. Followed by another and another. Through each one, she tried deep-breathing; she drank water. None of it mattered because I'd come for her. And I wouldn't leave unrequited.

She took her fourth period class to the library. They had to walk from the trailer classroom of her every day to the behemoth and overcrowded main building. The walk buoyed her. The cool spring air felt good; she lifted her head, twisting it this way and that to catch the slight breeze. It masked the sweating; she breathed it in. She smiled because she thought she'd won. I followed them inside.

She'd arranged a reprieve before she knew she'd need one. The librarian would do most of the work, book talks, book selections, book check-outs. She could sit and concentrate on deep-breathing, on meditation, on water. But I didn't leave. I remained undeterred, smiling in my own way that most people don't understand.

The sweat dripped now and pooled under her clothes. She shivered. She gripped her folder and smeared finger stains. She fought; I'll give her that. But, I knew I'd win.

I always win.

When she opened her eyes and picked up her head, she found her folder on the floor and the school nurse searching for her pulse. Colleagues, proficient with defibrillator paddles, ringed her. The students had gone; her department chair came in.

She pleaded; she wheedled, but she was as convincing as a threadbare used-car salesman, and I realized she'd be taken to the hospital. The others would insist. Her doctor insisted, over the phone. It would make my job harder, but certainly not impossible.

She brought stacks of papers with her, thinking she'd complete them from her hospital bed. A nurse made her put them aside; they caused her to sweat again. Her heart rate to jump.
They hooked up drips and machines. They chastised her for going in to work that morning. They wheeled her to a room in a familiar unit where banks of monitors nestled in the walls. Anyone passing could watch the green lines, my green lines, form hills and valleys, peaks and spikes, flats. I fondled those screens.

Her nurse came in and hung another bag to drip, drip, drip. Medication to slow her down, stop the sweating, stop the racing.

Even though I'd followed her to this room; even though I still watched from the corner; she paid no attention to me. I smiled and attended her machines and gazed at the drip.

She got her papers back and worked on them; the nurse checked her machines. The doctors increased the drip.

They kept her. Overnight and overnight. She sat awake watching television shows she didn't know existed. Machines belted harmonies with each other and florescent lights tap danced off the shining floor tiles. No one can rest in the middle of a nightly Mardi Gras parade. They do accommodate my purposes, however, so I don't complain.

People came: doctors, family, friends. I stayed in the corner, biding my time. Drip. She'd nearly finished the papers she'd brought and fretted about falling behind; she dreaded being left with only the television's poor amusement.

No visitors came in the third morning. She had a lull between temperature monitorings, so she picked up the last of her papers and rode the bed to an upright position. I slipped from my corner perch and looked over her shoulder at the handwritten teenage essays. I smiled at their concentrated, tongue-biting efforts; they tried, bless them. I glanced at her chirping monitor, slower now despite untangling indecipherable student handwriting. Drip. I rubbed her neck, and she twisted it with a sigh. Shhh. My fingers made circles on her temples, and her eyes felt heavy and drooped. Drip. I slipped my hands inside her brain, and she laid the essays in her lap. Shhh. Don't fight. You need sleep. Drip. Close your eyes. Just for a minute. Shhh.

Still, she fought. Of course she did; she's stubborn. She gulped in air; she forced her eyes to widen; she snapped her head up. But, I can be patient, and persuasive. Shhh. I whispered in her ear a new-mown grass scent, the sound of jeweled sunshine. I kneaded, I massaged, I soothed. I beckoned, and she followed without realizing I'd won.

I showed her my world. Silent—despite the machine's shrieking. Peaceful—despite the busyness of the hall. But the best part, the best part was the power to breathe deep, into the lungs, into the muscles, into the mind. The best part was the release from constraint, tension, worry; she inhaled the giddy, springtime freedom of it.

She stopped fighting; I'd won her over. She tasted the quiet darkness and nestled into the embrace of the peace, the release. Washing over her like warm waves in a gentle ocean. Like a cashmere blanket pulled up. Like the arms of a tender lover. I longed for her to stay; she reached for me, as Adam reached for the hand of God. But couldn't quite touch.

Her eyes opened against her will. She wondered at the machine with the red background and the large, yellowish zero. She blinked and blinked again and glanced out the window at the liquid-blue April sky. Then, she heard. She heard a rush and a push at her door. She turned her head to watch the nursing staff, eyes big as soccer balls, cram into the room. She told me they reminded her of the Keystone Cops, all trying to get into a too-small space at once. And with sentient thought, I knew I'd lost her.

The machine stopped shrieking and the zero became thirty. The nurses called the doctors, and the doctors stopped the drip. Mon amour, the drip.

The nurses took away her grading and lowered her bed, falsely believing mere pieces of paper could accomplish what only I can. I huffed, indignant at their presumption. They shoved me aside. But, she considered me as I lingered in her doorway, and the corners of her mouth turned down. She didn't speak out loud, but she offered to come with me. Too late. Our moment had passed.

A young doctor she hadn't seen before came in and sat by her bed. "Well. That was impressive." She smiled and leaned over and listened and asked if that had ever happened before. She sent in her senior. A wiry man with gray hair tufting all over his head and wire-rimmed glasses that matched his body type, the embodiment of quiet authority.

"Did I die?"

He paused and looked grave, placing a hand on the bedrail, "Yes."

"Huh." She thought a minute, then grinned, "I could use this to my advantage."

He wrinkled his brow and left.

They sent her away from the hospital, and two days later, she stood in front of her classroom honestly answering the teenagers' questions, a balm to their fears. Her eyes wandered to the back corner. My corner. I lounged on her bookshelf, leaning against the wall with the *Harry Potter* poster. The one from the *Deathly Hallows*. We locked eyes, appreciating the irony.

Since then I've stayed around. Years now. Hovering. Always close by. 'She misses me,' I've told myself ever since her eyelids fluttered and she saw the zero. But I'm patient. I smile. She understands.

An Egret in Flight
Amanda Hurley

Every sunset reminds me that an ending can also be beautiful. As the golden glow of the fading sun warms the windows of the glasshouse, I feel I am seeing the day's end as if for the first time. There's a ray of light peering cautiously through the windows at the far end, illuminating the hothouse in a myriad of colors. The light seems to dance with tiny speckles of radiance as if the conservatory is a cut diamond, its facets awash with gleaming prisms.

I'm sure it's not me just imagining it; it's as if every plant in the greenhouse has turned on its axis to bathe a flower, a leaf in this sublime, glowing light. There's a rustle of movement so quiet it's soundless, a sixth sense that you can never quite witness with your eyes. A hellebore I could swear a moment ago was facing in another direction now stands to full attention, its white delicate petals quivering with energy; a mariposa lily turns cupped hands, its praying petals bronzed by the dying rays of light.

As the sun dips down behind the hills and shadows creep across the fields, the ghostly hand of twilight is a precursor of the night to come. Inside the greenhouse, flowers close and plants curl in on themselves, leaves are tightly budded away; like every night, we sleep when the light is gone.

There's an ache in my bones as I too settle in for the night. My old army cot stretches as I nestle into its familiar bulge, carved by decades of rest. The rough woolen blanket that I pull to my throat covers a body of loosened flesh, my skin baggy where once taut, sticky with disease. I am the third in my line to tend to the plants in this greenhouse. There are varieties here that are the descendants of seeds my grandfather smuggled with him on his return to Germany from Brazil, hidden in knots in the hand-embroidered handkerchiefs his mother had made for him during the war.

My grandfather. My father. Me.

There is another kind of twilight creeping over the nursery now; I have no family, no children to whom I can gift my own inheritance. When I am gone, so too will my glasshouse disappear.

I sleep then, my dreams mingling as always with those of the plants I tend. Like every night, I am sent on journeys to continents I will never explore. Images like photographs on a camera screen flicker before my eyes.

Click. The Mexican moonlight cactus unfurls long pink petals to reveal a soft, anemone-like center. A sweetened fragrance fills the air and a dozen grey whispery-feathered moths appear to feed on this one-night-only flower that tomorrow will be withered and gone.

Click. I am in a forgotten rainforest in China; lush undergrowth drips with moisture and strappy green leaves hide small, stolen treasures. My dream self, shrunk to the size of a bee, settles on a habenaria radiata; the orchid's delicate frayed flowers shaped like an egret in flight. In my mind's eye, the tiny white blossoms shiver and become alive, launch themselves like soft, silver rain. Petals beat unseen wings as the flowers hover in the air beside me.

Click. One egret follows as I return to the forests of my native Germany, her feathered wings tinkling as delicately as a glockenspiel amidst the gloaming of pine, spruce, beech, oak. I land on a soft moss that springs below my feet. The dark woods hum with danger; the wild-growing forest flowers are a poisoner's delight. I am home.

Click. Thirsty from the long flight, my winged companion settles on a wild-growing fuchskraut, a tall, freestanding foxglove. Its blooms, shaped like thimbles, are sprinkled with purple confetti, maiden's bonnets that hide secret chambers to entice a cautious bird inside.

"No! It's poisonous!" I cry in my dream, unable to fight through layers of sleep to prevent my friend from sending an inquiring beak into the plant's enticing bells. She drinks, my egret, and the nectar has an immediate effect. Her delicate feathered blooms shudder and fall; her petalled wings leave dust on my fingertips as they wither away.

Click.

I am awake, sitting upright on my army cot; the woolen blanket tumbled to the floor beside me. Even the air in the hothouse feels heavy and poisoned. I have always loved the ripe hummus aroma of my greenhouse; now it is cloying and heavy to my lungs. I push myself up and out of the cot, hastening to the heavy doors to pull them aside and let in great gulps of cool night air.

I do not want to be the one to disband the greenhouse; to sell each plant at a bargain price, to watch as my begonias, orchids, poinsettias are carried away to car boots lined with newspaper, stuffed into bicycle bags. To bear witness to the nursery emptied of plants, sacks bare of bulbs. The last of the spilled soil swept into a corner, the long-whiskered marks of the broom left behind in the dust. The hothouse, vacant of life, shrunken in its emptiness.

And me? My last remaining months of life - I shudder to think of the room in the nursing unit reserved in my name. The smell of disinfectant instead of potting mix, breakfast served on a sterile tray instead of plucked from a ripe cherry tomato bush, sweetened with freshly-cut chives.

There's a lightening in the sky now, the first brightness of the false dawn, the basic notes of the early morning songbirds. Unwittingly I remember that every beginning can also be beautiful. As I sit just outside the conservatory's main door waiting for the warmth of the day, I feel my grandfather, my father standing as if just behind me. Their solid gnarled hands rest on my shoulders, nails still clotted with earth, fingers calloused from work. It is enough, they seem to say.

On this day…
Jane Killingbeck

How does it happen that this, **this** evening when I, as usual, bring the car around to face the rusted- white, cast iron gates of my home, (in order to negotiate the narrow drive way between the pillars without losing a wing mirror) pause the book tape (a Benjamin Black novel that I am reluctant to leave), dip the head lights, and get out to open the gates; How does it happen that I forget to put the handbrake on?

This, **this** evening, I walk as usual across the road, carefully watching for approaching cars, before I undo the old multi-coloured dog lead I use to tie the gates closed, keeping the dogs safe, and gently push them open allowing the dogs to come and welcome me, jumping and yapping and wagging tails; and I feel a nudge to the back of my legs and turn, just as the car rolls gently into the gate post at my side, pushing me gently forward through the open gateway.

I am confused. I compute vaguely that I can't have put the handbrake on; I realise the car has just careened straight across the gently- cambered road from where I had parked it in the drive-way opposite, with the engine still on, rolling into the gate pillar and into the back of my legs. I am horrified at the thought of the consequences, if it had not hit the pillar, but continued to gain momentum to roll through the gate entrance, run me down , and possibly also hit one or other of the dogs, before coming to a halt somewhere in the garden; I turn and look down at the car bonnet in disbelief.

Then I realise I had better get back in and move the car, which is still partly on the road, so I gather the dogs safely into the back seat, and reverse back into the road, and then forward to quickly get through the narrow gates and into the garden before a car comes along; It is a long straight stretch of country road and sometimes cars hammer down there as if it was a racetrack.

I sit and listen to the end of the 5 minute section of my book-tape, absorbed in John Banville's incomparably beautiful prose and the 1950s Dublin he evokes, before turning off the engine. I don't immediately examine the front bumper, but go to open the door of my house, submitting to the usual joyous jumping welcome from Bella, my oldest dog, who stays in the house when I am gone, and to the renewed ecstatic yappings of Nellie, and clumsy boundings of Jack as they follow me from the car and into the living room. Only then I get the torch and go back out to see what damage had been done. Nothing at all, that I could see, my car being an already battered, scratched, bumped and hardly-gleaming white Toyota Starlet dating from 1998; but in the days since that incident, every now and then a more noticing person has commented on the dent in the bonnet, and I have told them this story, confirming their impression of me as an increasingly mad old woman.

Like my mother I suppose. Every time I go to stay with my 91 year old mother, I am concerned that she is still driving. I find ways to avoid driving with her for fear of sudden death. She will not hear of giving up, having managed to get her licence back after being diagnosed with epilepsy, and after an episode in the village when, due to a lapse in consciousness; a petit- mal as it is called, she managed to hit several trees along the side of the road, smashing up her car, but emerging unscathed, having most fortunately not hit anyone.

Unfortunately though, as she does not remember this happening, the full horror of what could have happened does not seem to have occurred to her, and so after the 2 years ban, and having been put on medication for the epilepsy, she was entitled to have her licence renewed. People in the village were horrified when she began driving again, but my mother seemed to be confident that she was perfectly able to continue, albeit only on the local roads she knows. Surreptitiously she has the numerous bumps and scratches which her car acquires due to her poor judgement concerning walls and hedges and bollards fixed by a local man whom she calls out frequently, then forgetting she has done so.

I am severely critical of my mother's inability to let go of driving a car, but I must ruefully acknowledge that my own children probably begin already to have misgivings about my driving capabilities, when they hear stories such as that related above. I am perhaps my mother in more ways than I like to admit.

Capsized
Jill Ocone

I take my first steps into today's morning, and my feet are immediately submerged.

The water rises second by second.

The sharks circle and snap at my legs as a jellyfish entangles my ankles with his long, slimy tentacles.

He stings my skin something fierce, the discomfort sears deep to my core.

The water, it reaches my neck as I attempt to steady myself, but the swift-moving current knocks me off balance.

A blue-claw crab with a hint of yellow threaded through its pinchers pinches my fingers as I struggle to stay afloat, but it's not enough.

I'm not enough.

I desperately flail my arms, but the tide is too fierce.

I furiously kick my feet, but the water is too thick to tread.

I scream for a lifeline, but instead, impractical directives are haphazardly imparted to me from a blindness on high.

Swim faster!

Move quicker!

Try harder!

My head inevitably goes under.

I sink ever so slowly before the full force of the ocean drags me downward.

Trapped.

I'm trapped and I'm drowning.

The water is dense in my lungs and I fail to stay afloat.

I fail.

The gulls, they mock me in unison as they take flight in every direction with no regard for my existence.

Along comes the octopus who glowers as he pummels my torso with each of his heavy-foot legs. After three cycles of strikes, he disappears into the background, but he is never really gone.

I am breathless… depleted… abandoned by all except for the sharks who feed on my flesh and the jellyfish who intensifies his sting.

Just as I begin to black out, a surge arrives from nowhere and heaves me onshore.

I crawl, gasping and spent, then unsteadily gain my footing on the saturated sand.

I survive.

I weep as I drift asleep only to become submerged again by the vast ocean of unsustainability with my first steps into tomorrow's morning.

The Shapeshifters
Catherine Kim

엄마, 떠날 때 저를 데리고가주세요.

For you, her mother said. I've stayed for you; I've done everything for you—

For a moment, as Yeou rubbed the sleep from her eyes with the back of her wrists, she was surprised at the touch of her flesh over the bone, though if the stranger in her reflection on the window had asked her why, the thought might have wriggled out of her ear with a 짹짹! and taken flight, and there would have been nothing to see in the glass save for the child overlaid the lake of grass held back by the smear of the road. The stranger must have known this, as she settled back into alignment with Yeou's eyes and kept her otherworldly secrets to herself, which meant the unfamiliarity of Yeou's small and naked wrists remained squirming in the nest of her skull, feathers wet with grey matter.

그 끔찍한 소리가 들리나요? Her mother pulled the van over to the side of the road, and the scrape of something hard and heavy against the asphalt stuttered to a stop with the vehicle. Yeou climbed over the rim of the backseat into the trunk and pressed her face against the glass, as her mother squatted on the road behind the car and bent her trunk so her crown could peer underneath. Yeou couldn't see the branches growing over the undercarriage, or the pretty bulbs that bloomed into milky eyes with pale coronas encircling their wrinkled pits, so she licked the stranger on the nose to ask her what she saw, for surely, the ghost could see her mother with a head having grown as big as the road behind her. The stranger flicked her on the nose, and wings fluttered over the bars of Yeou's ribcage, and the child must never cry, so she scrunched up her face and smacked her head on the glass of the wicked woman's head. 쿵! Her mother stumbled out of the underworld, a hand cradling the quickening bruise on the back of her head, and as she rapped her knuckles on the windshield, her angry features overlaid the shrinking ghost. The feathered organ writhed in Yeou's chest, digging through her bones with its terrible beak, so she ducked out of sight and scurried back to her seat, ears flat against her head and the pads of her paws darkening her sight.

A game to pass the time in which the father in the sky, who is not the father on Earth who is coming ever closer which is why mother has them sleep in the car and drive for so long, who is not that father yet but the one that has her mother flip the visor over the windshield as he says goodbye, hides his face in his hands and has Yeou guess where he's gone. Has he slipped under a cloud or behind a mountain or in the curtain of her mother's hair on one of their few good days? Is he trapped in the amber of a bottle with the tempest, or in the static of the man on the radio who says he saw his wife vanish before his eyes, saw his child grow tails and scamper outside— oh, there's the evening sun! 까꿍! There's the happy moon. There's the sunshine, or the moonbeams, which is the dragon spinning round and round the wish-fulfilling jewel. The stranger in the window rubbed the fur at the nape of Yeou's neck with her knuckle-bones as she startled the bees from her mother's sweetling cheeks with her laughter: ㅋㅋㅋ!

She must have eaten a bird. The thought had her lick her jowls. It had been pecking at the dip of her mother's temple, scattering sap over her pretty blouse, gobbling up the squirming meal it found burrowed in the wood. Her father had tried birdwatching, once. His friend, who'd gone into the military before him, only to have fled into the mountains and shot himself, had known the names of all the birds in the sky. Her father found he hadn't the patience for it, thought Yeou
might be better at it, would have told her soon so she'd know that birds were good and sometimes people leave you and it's not your fault, if her mother hadn't made like a bird and left. How strange, she never knew that trees could uproot themselves, that leaves could catch the air, that good mothers bled flower petals from their eyes. If she dug her fingers into her plump car seat she might feel the bark running underneath, though surely if she did the bird she had eaten would peck its way out of her stomach and collapse into the wreck of her lap, and there would be nothing to see in the glass but the child overlaid the mountainsides bound taut by the smear of the road, and the seat cushion would be a seat cushion and her mother would shrink into a human again to say they were turning back, so instead Yeou stretched her paws as she yawned with all her teeth and did not dig her claws into her car seat and unwound herself as the stranger in the window gave her ears a scratch before sinking it back into the meat of the big, soft walnut in her skull, riddled as it was with bird bites.

Dixie
Kate E Lore

I once worked at a call center. It was stuck right in the middle of a long line of business offices on Dixie road. It looked clean and neat like a doctor's office when you first entered through the front door. Going back, down the hallway, you'd find a bunch of people behind glass each one in front of a computer, on a telephone, writing things down and reading from a printed paper script.

You don't really realize how quiet the hallway is, because of the soundproof walls, until you experience the shock of noise that hits you upon opening the door. The cubicles are wood painted pale blue, cheaply made. The computers are shockingly old, boxy things with telephones built into the side connected by wire. They don't ring. They blink green. The manager explained to me, on the first day, that there had been a recent break in and all of their good computers had been stolen. This was Dixie road after all.

There was air conditioning only in the first office. The calling area had several large fans that contributed to the noise. We were given two smoke breaks and a lunch. We worked from 9-7 Monday through Thursday and then only 9-3 on Fridays. The seats were metal fold-up. I remember my back always hurt when I worked there.

I'd found out about the job from a girl I'd worked with at McDonalds. I had been trying and trying but couldn't get a job anywhere. I have found, in the city of Dayton where the economy could certainly be doing better, it to be near impossible to get a job without knowing someone. And this was after McDonalds, after several jobs, after dropping out of college, after my second waitressing job had been lost due to the business selling.

I'd never really thought much about my city defining who I am and shaping certain aspects of my life until after I moved here. It takes the distance of living somewhere else to truly see a place maybe. But it makes the changes harder. Where building and street renovations used to be an easy switch they now seem like strange ugly alterations to the places I remember.

Back when I lived there I'd found my life in Dayton to be something of a repeating pattern. Certain things just kept coming up. Like Dixie road for example. My Father had lived on North Dixie road in a small, plain, hardly furnished apartment. He didn't have cable so we played cards. We played rummy. We sat on plastic yard chairs at a round table. We played the original super Mario bros on Nintendo. The television sat on a milk crate. He'd lived off the same street, Dixie, maybe four miles away, in a decent condo with his girlfriend many years later. While writing for Dayton City Paper I got to interview strippers in a strip club located on North Dixie road, one parking lot away from where I stood in my fathers-girlfriend's-ice cream truck watching my father get arrested for posession.

I have watched the premier of a Harry Potter movie at a drive in theatre located on North Dixie and stayed for the second showing so that we drove home under the sunrise. It was beautiful. I have gone to a party in the same condo housing located off Dixie road where my father once lived, and I have ended up swimming in my underwear in the same pond from which I once caught a fish.

I have purchased pot in a parking lot on North Dixie road. I once caught a wild kitten at my dad's-girlfriends-parents house, and yes they too lived on Dixie.

I once had a pet box turtle. My brother had come home with her. Round domed shell, dented in the front from, probably, a car. I named her Dixie after the road from which he had found her.

I loved Dixie. I made her a pen in the back yard that was three feet across and six feet long. She had sheltered space, open space, and a water box that was changed to fresh water every day. I would let her crawl around in the back yard for half an hour or more at least once every day. That is, except for when it was cold, and she hibernated buried under leaves and dirt later relocated to the safety of my bedroom, still buried but less cold.

But what I never understood was why Dixie always tried to escape. She was always digging at the chicken wire fence. Always testing the strength of her fortifications. Dixie did run away too. The first time was under the fence. I got her back. My friends found her half way around the block a day later. The second time she climbed over the fence. I did not get her back.

I learned later in life, from a friend who worked at a wild life rescue, that box turtles are naturally drawn to where they were born. That they will always try to go in that direction, that they have a natural compass for home.

This makes me wonder just how far Dixie got. Makes me wonder if North Dixie road is really where she was from or had we interrupted her previously started journey. What if she'd already travelled miles and miles finally reaching North Dixie when my brother found her? Box turtles have a possible life span of up to eighty years. She could still be out there. Or she could have been seventy when I met her. Maybe she's roamed the country, covered more miles than me, looking for a field of grass where now a shopping mall stands. She could be looking for a home which no longer exists. Maybe she accidentally walked past it because she didn't recognize home. Maybe one of these days I'm going to drive right past Dayton, not recognize it, and just keep going.

Drops
Lisa Rosenblatt

"I can't do it," she says... pacing back and forth on the wooden floor.

He takes one slightly cupped hand and presses it to her ear, presses close and paces with her in rhythm, whispering "better to hear you with my dear." She giggles from his words tickling her ear, of course, and pushes his hand away.

No matter how hard he tries to break her pacing, wag a finger, block her path, she remains unfazed, brushes him and his gestures aside, and blurts out, "Do not even think that it has anything to do with you."

It doesn't and he knows it.

"You want to give up? Just give up," he glares dramatically, while at the same time, making sure she sees, points toward the door. "You really want to give up? well just walk out that door; you really, truly want to leave, give up? well go and do it. I'm finished waiting for you," he says.

That's it. That's all there is to it. Her feet pacing, the static, and bang, the slam of a door.

The dogs bark, jump around, splash and stick their noses in when I throw rocks in. Honey, you've got to bring it back. She throws rocks in for as long as she can. "This is the last rock I will throw," she says.

"Watch now, stick your face in, splash that water, face in with an intensity of purpose, emerging with a rock, usually a very big one, as you think that I will be pleased to see a very big rock and the mixture of moistures and saliva dripping down from your muzzle." Knowing full well that the dogs have forgotten that the point is to pull out the rock that she threw, laughing, she throws another, forgetting that she said the last would be the last...

The mountain stream begins with snowfall. I will find that source of snowfall. The mountain peaks still cling steadfast to clumps of snow. Snow that was once fresh, that made its presence as the snow of deep winter, now crusting, old, enhancing the greenness of the valley.

She crumples up the bit of paper and tosses it.
I empty out my pockets and arrange the contents on the table. They are my pockets, damn it. I do not remember where this string comes from. This piece of string, this crumpled wrapper, and this tissue. A crumpled tissue, more lint. The sun is shining.

And he sits on the chair and places his briefcase on the table, roughly a hands-width away in front of him, and coughs. He scans the hands of the woman across from him. She has a ring on her pinkie finger. *She just wants to get home, just wants to leave,* but he starts up a conversation. "I'm glad you're here," he says, staring at her pinkie. She glances up, "it does not mean anything." He rests his elbows on the table, entwines his fingers and puts his chin on the backs of his entwined fingers, leaning forward using his hands like a little hammock for his chin – pressing his face close, crunching up the corners of his eyes making the tiny wrinkle lines on his cheekbone peaks dance, and says, "I must tell you, though, it does. I'm sure it does, it has to."

She tosses another. The dogs always want more.

He sits in the office reading the day's mail. He contemplates the sandwich that he put in his briefcase early that morning, the crispness of lettuce, the tick of the clock on the wall, and coffee. He pushes the knot of his tie from side to side, loosening it around his neck, and then lets his hands fall.

"Make it quick," I say, it's raining. Something bangs. I believe it is her heart. I meant to write *head* here, not *heart*.

    It begins to rain. Yes, of course, dogs always want more. I must take shelter somewhere. please let me in, it's pouring.
    He is standing on one leg. Balancing. He asks if I am from the post office. I say, "Are you kidding?"
That is my table! I'm not sure why – but... we always played cards together – she points to the middle of the page – I have to wipe the table, wash the glasses, organize the trash, there are crumbs on the table. I wipe them away and then they come back. And it is still raining.

I think that she has no idea. No one ever seems to.

Just to listen, I tease her.

She writes home.

 I start all over again. I promise. Ready or not?

The wind licks my face, it is gentle and strong and warm. I reach down to pick up another stone. The wind whips a strand of hair against my face. The rain begins to fall.

We are lying on the lawn with our hands intertwined, the soil is moist, its warmth seeps through our T-shirts, as we stare up at the sky. He is out on the street tossing hoops. Boom. Swoosh. Boom. Boom.

Animals at Work: a short + a poem
Tiffany Lindfield

Trapped

Triche let the screen door flap violently. She slammed it, again, so hard it boomeranged, and she slammed it again. She could've torn that damn door right off the hinges. She imagined flinging it so high, and so far, that it went over the tall oak fence tracing her back yard; a yard empty of everything but grass, now turning a bright green. Instead, she squatted on the ground, caving her face into her hands, weeping hard, for a life unlived, for what should've been, wept for the misery that had defined her life—and wept because her marriage was so unhappy.

"I'm leaving him," she said out loud, through her teeth, gritted so hard that bone dust accumulated in the side pockets of her mouth; she spat it out beside her.

When the sun rose in the sky, tickling the yard with rays of light, she lifted her eyes, mistrustful at first, like raccoons leaving dens at dusk. And there on the fence post sat a red Cardinal singing its heart out. The birdfeeder was empty. Beyond empty; it was rusted. She pulled it from the shepherd's hook and scrubbed it clean. She tossed canned goods around in the cupboard but there wasn't anything to feed a bird.

At the local grocery, she stared at the shelves stacked with bird seed. So many choices. Were there this many birds, and did they all eat different things? A short woman rang her up with glittery nails so long they curled under. Triche tilted her head, wondering how much stuff could get caught under spoons for nails.

"You got birds?" the woman asked.

"A red Cardinal."

"He gonna be eatin' for a year." The woman bagged several feeders and bags of seed.

Triche screwed hooks into the fence. She plunged the spiked end of shepherd hooks into dry dirt, pretending the dirt was her own wrist; the roots stubborn, unlike the fragile blue veins that peeked from under her skin.

She hung the feeders of all sorts: Basket feeders, tube feeders, hopper feeders and more. The original feeder—a mason jar feeder—was now lost in the crowd. Triche squatted down on the ground and watched for the Cardinal. She watched so long that she got hot from the spring heat, and realized the birds would need water, too. "A bird bath," she said, an eureka moment with a voice sure, and sturdy.

A hippie ran the local nursery. He wore a diamond earring in one ear, talking in a demanding voice. He told her that if she wanted birds, she would need insects. He talked a blue streak about the web of life, and how humans had messed it all up. He helped her load pots of pollinators, and other flowers meant to attract bees, butterflies, and the like. Dirt, too, and gloves. All this sat alongside a terracotta bird bath in the back of her car, equipped with a fountain.

The sun was an hour from setting, and she was exhausted, but kept working. Her back ached, and she kept digging holes for the new flowers and arranged some in pots. Finally, with sweat dripping down the arch of her back, into the crease of her pants, she squatted. *"And Triche made the yard in seven hours,"* she puttered, her stomach growling for food.

Oddly, it felt good. The hunger. The ache in her bones made her remember them again, made her feel alive. She crawled in bed, savoring the feel of the vertebrae in her spine, the itch of the mosquito bites on her legs, and the bread barely touching the acid in her stomach. And then she remembered, "Hummingbirds need to eat, too!"

She rolled over in the bed with her phone, pulling up Amazon.

Her husband elbowed her hard. "I'm trying to sleep."

She got out of bed, went into the yard, and pressed her bare feet on the ground still wet from having been watered, ordering paradise for hummingbirds.

"Somewhere for me to sit and watch the birds," she said, ordering a wrought iron table and a chair set for the patio.

<<>>

Triche sat proudly. and comfortably now that the wrought iron chairs were adorned with soft cushions. The sun was about to rise, and she was front and center with a cup of cold tea in one hand, and a marijuana joint in the other. She sat there for hours, watching Yellow Finches squeeze Nyjer seed from a mesh sack, an American Robin stress over two fledglings, the Monarchs devouring Milkweed, and the bees nuzzling their heads so far into sunflower blooms that their legs became caked in yellow. She imagined her fingers dipped in lemon icing; her face submerged into the crease of someone who cared about her.

She lit the joint and focused her mind on the feet of the bees with their faces buried deep into the armpit of flowers, into the belly of their lovers. She focused on the sunflowers, loving the tallness of their stalks, their spring faces that had upturned to the sky, now their summer faces in full bloom. She knew their fall faces would bow beautifully. She loved the grasshoppers that nibbled their leaves, and the beaks of birds on their crowns.

She watched the Ruby-Throated Hummingbirds and Yellow Jackets fight each other over nozzles of sugar, and Blister Beetles swarm the small flowers of Mountain Mint. All this made her forget her heart ache.

"I'm gonna leave his ass before summer ends," she said aloud to the Lantanas falling out of pots, and to the Crepe Myrtle's bounty of pink and purple blossom's spilling from small buds.

Then fall came, and she set up a squirrel feeding station. A chipmunk she aptly named Chip would eat from her hand, and a family of raccoons would depend on her harvest to make it through winter's hibernation. Even a growing deer, orphaned, aptly named Bambi, nippled milk from a bottle she prepared every morning and noon. Sweet Potato vines ran up two lattices she found at a yard-sale and had painted sea green. The summer sun had traded Shasta Daisies and Black-Eyed Susans for Marigolds and Cosmos.

"I'll leave him when the Marigolds die," she said.

And then winter came, and the Witch Hazel bloomed, reminding her of sea urchins, Snow Drops peeked from a light blanket of snow in satin dresses while Viola's blasted her senses in deep purples and blues. The birds flocked to the feeders still promising spring's harvest, even in winter. The squirrels would awaken from long winter naps for fresh corn, and sunflower suet. The bird bath needed a warmer, and the house built for Bambi needed straw.

Triche shivered. "Too cold to move. I'll leave him in spring."

<<>>

He stepped outside, looking for her, contempt in his voice. She didn't answer. Her hair had become tangled in the climbing rose vines; her feet morphed into the pine needles that had fallen from the two evergreens east of the yard. Her hands remained rooted in the Weeping Willow. Her face had drowned in the small pond for the raccoons to dip their paws, and her legs had morphed into the prickly branches of black-berry bushes, and her stomach cast into the compost pit.

He walked inside, and her lips bubbled from the pond water, thick with algae, "I'm trapped."

Animals in the Snow
We were strolling in the woods and she said,
"Aren't we so lucky to be walking in the forest while it's snowing?"
And I pondered a moment. Lucky because we were bundled up,
Lucky because this was just a 'walk,' not a treacherous trek for survival.
'Yeah, we are," I replied seeing a break in the trees, a pasture of white in the distance,
 And our hearts raptured in joy.
I threw my hands up. "It's like we're trapped in a snow globe."
She said, like a child would say, "I love snow globes."
In the pasture three deer caught our scent, and we stopped to admire them,
Their big brown eyes, flakes of snow on their muzzles, catching on long black lashes.
Soft white tails flickering, white as the snowflakes falling in billowy puffs of pretty,
Catching on limbs, and she said, "it's so pretty how snow brings out all the branches."
Like eyeliner on the lids of eyes, I thought.
"Oh, I just want it to fall and fall and make a big white blanket, and we can curl under it!"
"We'll need pillows, too," she said, then the Buddhist in her remembered something:

"It will melt. Like everything melts. But right now, it's here."

THE HUMAN KIND
Evelyn Sharenov

Mayor Willy Wilson, CPA, rode Easy Gal at a slow trot down Main Street. Willy was gentle with Easy Gal. He placed a thick soft blanket under her saddle and whispered to his horse as they clopped down the cobblestones. Easy Gal's heavy head moved up and down and side to side. She listened and understood Mayor Willy who didn't want the old cobblestones to hurt Easy Gal's aging hooves.

Sandy River, Oregon in the Pacific Northwest drew people from the cities. They were starved for wildlife and birdsong, waterfalls, rivers and trees. They wanted a full five-sense complement of experiences. Fresh air and elbow room would clear their minds of the hustle of workday dirt, bricks, and the constant building in the big city.

More Fords made their way to the river towns, showy symbols of their success. The town folk didn't much care for the dust and dirt they raised on their way up the narrow curving roads, to the country they knew was there, up through the dense forests, early mists and fog to the row of waterfalls, each higher than the one before. Then they drove through an invisible barrier and the air was suddenly clear. They counted the waterfalls with growing excitement as the road led inevitably upward. When they reached the wild rush of icy water from the widest fall, the Multnomah, they all sighed. "Aaah."

They parked walking distance from the Falls and everyone stepped out of their cars to pose for photographs. It was like a shot of the strongest gin for them.

The Fords drove home around the Mayor and Easy Gal. They tipped their hats and puffed their cigars. The locals, hapless, jobless afternoon drinkers avoided the tourists who took lunch in the local bars and went home happy. The towns were home for a fair number of alcoholics and eccentrics who gave up their barstools for the visitors to Sandy River. They were grateful for the dark corners of the saloon on weekends, grateful to avoid the tourists and city folk. No one who lived there paid attention to prohibition in the first place. Now booze was legal again and the saloon made a fortune. It received weekly deliveries of good whiskey and gin. Willy figured pubs would spring up in time to serve all comers. Weekdays, the drinkers returned to their barstools.

The good townfolk elected Mayor Willy Wilson, CPA and then re-elected him. He was popular, friendly with neighbors, visitors and voters alike with whom he often shared a beers and stories. He rode Easy Gal and admired the changes he'd brought about since he'd taken office.

Neighbors always stopped and waved to the Mayor and his horse. They waved and Mayor Willy Wilson was happy with what he saw. Easy Gal was well known to the town-folk for her auburn beauty. She tossed her head so her glossy red mane attracted attention to her movie star looks.

The job of mayor was unsalaried. Willy didn't mind. He had enough money in the bank to live well. Today he'd left his usual workday in accounting to make sure they would be ready for the annual parade. This year he would formally unveil a sculpture. Two dolphins embraced as they rose out of a pond in a green space created solely for them. They were copper with a turquoise patina that curved down their back. The sunshine blessed them and exploded into brilliant lights. Stories went that the shards of broken sunshine could pierce your eyes and leave you blind if you weren't careful. You never stared directly at the sun and you didn't stare directly at the dolphins.

Mayor Willy dismounted Easy Gal. They clopped together down the cobblestones of Main Street which had been a dirt road just a couple of decades earlier. The cobblestones were attractive, easier on the eyes but harder on legs. The paved streets brought more tourists on foot. As penance for the cobblestones, Willy planned to pave the roads that year. Willy felt bad for the men and what the war did to them and their wives and children. He planned town improvements to provide jobs and a living wage for the men and their families, all those who paid the price of serving their country in the war to end all wars.

The work of putting down new streets would begin as soon as the summer festivals were over. Main Street was the straightest line to the saloon, the hub of the town's business. It would be first.

The Columbia River was to his to his left and the Sandy River to his right. From where he stood, the mayor had a clear view of both rivers. The Mayor believed he could fly a paper airplane with ease from one river to the other.

The Columbia River ran through a gorge that could suddenly blow winds that would knock you over if you weren't expecting them. A large grassland ran between the rivers and an old railroad ran on tracks in the middle of it all. When the railroad came out of a natural ravine to its first stop in town, what everyone saw first was red paint on the side of the first car. In bold letters it asserted THE END IS NEAR. After the war to end all wars, that was easy to believe. The railroad's route was limited, from north of Portland to the end of its run in Sandy, a scenic trip and convenient for some folk. On a map, all the rivers and towns were a pleasing arrangement of forest, water, and small inviting places to live, but the Sandy River was the most popular. It was the easiest of all the rivers to follow up to the waterfalls that ended in the mighty Multnomah. On a map it resembled a tangle of veins and arteries. At least that was the way Mayor Willy saw it. All that clear cold water spilled into the Columbia River.

The mayor hitched his horse to a wooden post built for the purpose, and walked into the saloon.

"Hey, Mayor Willy," the bartender called. "That statue is something to celebrate. Beer's on us. Anything new in town we need to know about?"

"No. I'll be happy when the tourists go back home and I can relax."

Willy knew everyone by name. A tap beer was ready for him and he swallowed it in a couple of gulps, talked up his old friends, got gossip he wouldn't otherwise hear, then knocked back another beer and continued on his way.

Small towns were an acquired taste. He loved it here. Some people didn't stay long enough to unpack, not with the Columbia Gorge winds and all. The sturdiest of the newcomers adjusted to the weather, bought homes with some land and dug in for the long haul.

The mayor was grateful for the spring day he'd chosen for this chance to oversee his town. It wasn't quaint or artsy but Mayor Willy had a vision for the town. The vision called for more pubs, restaurants with the cuisine of other countries, art galleries, a bookstore – especially a book store, where readers could sit and enjoy the written word.

That day he wore an old oiled duster and broken-in cowboy boots. He was lost in thought when an unexpected squall came roaring through the gorge. Had he been listening he would have heard the warning caws of the murder of crows. The wind hit him and everything in its path head on. Easy Gal kept her head down and away. Trees went flying and the world howled as the squall hurtled down the backbone of the gorge.

Then the wind travelled up through the mayor's coat, the lining of which was strapped to his legs. But his coat wasn't sewn for such for untoward events as what came at him at that moment. The coat filled with cold air and lifted him into the sky. He could see the street below and his friends grew smaller the higher he flew.

"By god, I'm flying." He was joyous, laughing out loud. He held his arms out to the side and felt the supreme pleasure of being airborne. There were nights when he dreamed he was flying, but knew that had something or other to do with sex. There were a couple of town legends of getting caught up in the gorge winds, but those were legends, not fact.

He quickly learned how to maneuver out over the Sandy River, arms out at his sides, legs lifted on drafts of cold air. He turned to the Columbia and then back again toward town. He was surprised to see he was not alone up there. Clouds of starlings flew like curling waves of ocean in the sky. They blanketed that part of the world in darkness. Their wings filled his head with a symphony of susurrus. It was a breathtaking show that mesmerized the mayor. He'd seen what he wanted – the rivers where the confluence of meteorology, geology and haberdashery met and took you out to the ocean if you weren't careful. He was turned and moved by the wind, happy now to be over dry land.

Then the squall stopped. The mayor dropped to the ground. He skittered over the cobblestones, then fell over, face down. Everyone who'd stopped what they were doing to watch the spectacle of their mayor's flight, turned their attention to the mayor lying prone in the middle of the street. When the mayor didn't move, a physician who practiced in the new hospital a couple of miles away, left his drink on the bar and ran into the street to see what the problem was.

"There's nothing to be done," he said.

The mayor was dead. The silent mutiny in the chest of a middle aged man. Everyone who saw the mayor splayed out like this, understood the outcome of the squall that stopped too soon.

Easy Gal reared up to her full height on her hind legs and kicked at the air with her forelegs. She cried in anguish when they took his body away. She tugged on her reins until they gave way. The sound of that horse weeping buried itself so deep in the soul of the townfolk they never forgot it. They wept when they thought of Easy Gal's grief.

She freed herself from the hitching post and followed the medic truck to the hospital where the Mayor's body was taken. She waited for him until she knew he wasn't coming back to her, then galloped off. All anyone saw of her after that was her auburn mane and tail flying behind her. She ran until she was exhausted from looking for her best friend. She was tired and thirsty, hopeless, but continued at a slow gait. She stopped finally at a pasture that called her into its world, for water, for apples, for soft grass. A quiet farmer came out to greet her. He didn't know what had happened in town but he knew this horse was grieving. He stroked her head, combed her forelocks with his fingers, and whispered that she could rest there with him, the she would be all right, that he would love her. He was kind.

"You're beautiful. Why are you so sad? You could be a movie star, you're that beautiful." He smiled at her. She shook her head up and down. Easy Gal didn't understand a word of it except that it was good. Up and down, she brought her heavy head. She rubbed her downy jaw against the farmer's cheek. He believed her arrival was meant to be, so he invited her to stay and showed her to a stall, clean, with sweet hay, blankets, everything a sad horse, a horse that had lost her love, needed.

"I do believe this place was meant for you," the farmer told Easy Gal.

The mayor's death briefly occupied the town's imagination. The mayor's body was buried simply, and a small but heartfelt funeral held for a small-town mayor and accountant. But it was the sound of that horse, her cry that everyone took home with them that day.

The farmer felt awful for this horse, so he stretched out next to her in the hay and they slept together until bright sunshine between the wood slats of the barn awakened them.

Whoever would obliterate1 it from me, in exchange for that end which I am searching for in vain, would h[er]self become my [...] In darkness, [s]he would see me: my word would be h[er] silence, and [...]

———*Maurice Blanchot,*
translated by Lydia Davis

Prologue to a Longer Something Else
煦 **(Susie Zhu)**

[and above all, transcribed (ir)responsibly]
by Susie (Xu) Zhu,

who is reading Blanchot at the moment, in a place where she once spoke only Chinese but felt inextricably foreign, found English *all Greek* and *French du chinois.*

1

"But you know, I am only *wood*."
"No you are not. At least you are a *tree*."

"And at most?"

I want to say, *woods, my darling, of course*. But she who has no body could not stand long enough for the treat, fell flat **behind the wall²**.   Still

life, a wet stretched shadow I trailed ever after the first sight into water.

2

is a hallway of absolute negative space, undulating
far off into
into

and into

into too much
into

that could never then be returned
into
the flipping pages once hold dear with much naivety

at one *entrance*³, I closed the door
of familiarity
but chopped into two by my looming anachronism.

3 : *that of* THE *house, or…?*

When did I finally forget remembering your face from mine?
She asks.

This house has been emptied by too many departures, now too flat to be articulated into an answer. Too lumbering to be mown. Deceives time too easily.

She asks me to take my time but how am I able to when it is all withheld to her side? Secret signals in pieces, table, chair, whispering to her many yesterdays that I read not. The same doormat yet with no welcome, the same fish tank with no fish, the same everything only but more teeming with

silence,
I could not find a word for her but I found plenty of silence.
Safe space to *swim*[4].

4

Instead of struggling I let gravity do and secretly head down aspired to learn to produce gills. The water tastes salty, in tired eyes, in ambiguity, the sound sleeps.

The remnant from my first haircut still lying in same claim on the same shelf, a snippet of past no more than a concept, a touch like someone else's, fingers, running through, tying into a different person.

Now, like night from any *window¹*, the dark silky fibers let go of their boundaries to converge, and I let go of mine.

5

The entire world sunk into deep sleep while time did not,
distorting everything as it swelled into a boiling pot of light.

She used to stay up just to witness how, like dawn injects night through that slit of
crescent, it spills into many salty gooey liquid dreams, and she'll watch in amazement
as they clotted and dropped like egg whites.

Appendix

When the door closed behind and air drains out, numb as lips soaked in absurd wishes. Dry. Is the world or what once was the world. Vast as it is could still be drown at a thin horizon. In a leaf but against a plain.

Day infers night but not anymore. Closeness, in its profundity. The house offers, and dispels. Swooning poor volatile creatures with the afternoon daze, so infinitely prolonged. My closeness, in its profundity, in its house.

When the door shall open but in the other direction? When

Water flow back again, I shall nest in the time built for me. That glass **vase**[6] standing absent among a glacier of years must still absorb and decipher the message else she'd starve to death. She stares, blankly into the unknown familiarity, not deja vu —— Something more tangible, sensual, like memory.

---

6 : A container without *Handle, itself*

I do not exist, do not know her until 8 years later when she returned, finally, once again, to our unity. Once again our hands aligned across the plane. Our faces overlaps into a timeless image.

We drew one line along the aged entryway wall, upon where it stretches slowly into a house-ful of text. Where it cracks, splits, and loses its reflectiveness. Once a mirror, now made into the cover, wrapping around our **piece***.

*

"Prologue to a Longer Something Else"

came out in late March, 2020, or in any other time attached to *it*.
To the house where *she* and the text was born.

(The transcriber, Susie, if you still remember, is in the same house. She has wasted an abundance of childhood in such a space and only just re-entered after 8 years of absence. All is saturated, including silence. In a duration of 14 days, all is within, and along the waterway in her whispering words, sent drifting away at once, out, radiant and diffusive, into the sparse knitting of re-re-re-re-re re-remembrance.)

essays.

Journal 11: Dendro-pomorphic
煦 (Susie Zhu)

Kids who give trees roots in their drawings alway make me nervous.

I have thought of this as a solid proof of my awkwardness with children in general but it turns out that it is this uncanny stylistic choice of portraying trees that's causing the unsettlement. The image of a tree with roots in dimensionless scape: There is an acuteness in such perception, regardless of age—though adults usually tend to obscure it. They draw with more prudent articulation, like layering. Adding even more confusion onto the tree so that its image starts to peel back like dark barks revealing the pristine core in soft sage colored gleam. Confused and confused until eventually the tree becomes totally depleted of complication, light and delightful. Delightful sap dripping down like honey. Sometimes when people stand in front of these drawings they say that's innocence. But it is in truth a camouflage. What they layer on top of their naked trunk is something fleshier. Like human faces or shoes. Occasionally garments as well.

Kids who give their tree roots are real dreamers (a term employed less as figurative language but rather seriously ethnological.)

And I have indeed, for once, met a boy who did that. It was during my residency at a kindergarten, in another country as far from my hometown as how a flip-side is from its front. I vaguely remember once making up my resume as a "Chinese antique-style garden designer" and sending it everywhere quite a long time ago—that must be what had gotten me there. She was also unemployed at the time and according to her theory "two must not be au chômage at once in any two-person relationship" I was made to accept the offer. I did not understand why she enjoyed mixing French words into conversations (with someone who does not speak French) so much as I still don't now. But I loved how the word sounds like cheese, so I chewed on that quite a bit on my trip to work. When I arrived, the person in charge informed me that the headmaster would like me to teach Art instead. Later there were rumors about the former instructor who had gotten a severe fever in her dream and was unlikely to return. From the coma? She'd fallen into it.

I wonder if it was the guilt of being dishonest...Somehow I decided to make the first assignment to draw a tree. And there was the boy, with emerald eyes of a cat (correction: whose eyes I then have all cats adopt in my fantasy, since I have never really looked into the eyes of a cat.) In his sketchbook, there was nothing but an

almost symmetrical tree floating on the page. A rather Giacomettish tree ambling in the air, unlike the other trees—which are more or less the same with one half dipped in the night soil and the other half exposed in wide daylight. I asked him if he could draw the earth like all his other peers, out of polite curiosity. He frowned for a while in silence as if pondering over an incredibly absurd request or some enigmatic questions, but he accepted anyway. He painted the entire page grey, thicker than a late winter mist except towards the bottom—far apart from the tree
—where he laid a thin tapestry of houses. There he pointed and said: earth.

What's so special about trees anyway? A tree absorbs images and has them emanate into every finest membrane of strata as air carries lights into visibility. When the images finally came to me, so was a devastating epiphany that I would be the only person seeing this. Despite all my effort. The moment I release my tightly clenched hands to record, the images flap their tiny wings and vanish back into the thick wet mist. Eventually I wrote: a tree is a mirror. And trees in the air?

So the roots are not the shadow of a tree but a tree existing twice. But duplicity is not allowed, people do not understand. So dreamers must hide, they must find the right device to protect themselves. So dreamers hide in the form of trees entwined with air, space, time or the lack of all of them pressing toward them from the surrounding, like true ardent lovers. Like lovers, yes—Lover is understood. But certainly a bit early for a 4-year-old. So I gave this boy a long, solid hug and whispered to his ears that he should, never again, draw trees at school. He looked at me once again perplexed.

The boy with his flying tree made me nervous, but not nearly as much as the others did. In fact, that whole place made me nervous. That slowly hardening concrete of beliefs in the whatsoever reality glaring in people's eyes made me nervous. The headmaster made me nervous—I have absolutely no idea why he wanted me there.

Is the umbilical outside or inside a body? Let the tree free. I don't think anyone should be accused for taking whichever side of the answer. If it is ever eligible for one. What is happening out there? Why are the exorcising lamps lighting up against the night drapes? Why so alerted? Why is everyone so silent in front of its offering? Is it another witch-hunt?

Musings During the Time of Covid-19 (or Unwinding the Mind)
Dan Mariani

In this baffling age of Covid one can't be sure of anything. The days' march on. The nights' march on. Quality of living has diminished. That we are sure of. We live in this new cage of fear. The rules of the game are constantly changing. Wear one mask, wear two masks, one over the other. Socially distance yourself, stay six feet apart, wash your hands vigorously, don't touch your face, Lysol the toilets, get fresh air, but not with other people. We have no idea who is harboring the virus. Keep a safe distance away, wash your clothes when coming back from Walmart, wipe down the grocery carts, take a bath in a solution of Mr. Clean *(don't do that)*. Rub your face down with Clorox, but don't drink it! Take Vitamin D, Pepcid also seems to help, Zinc too! Add to that, trying to figure out what vaccine is best for what phase of the disease with the lowest number of side effects! Not that you have a choice….

Walks in the park can be therapeutic. Except that there are scores of people doing the same thing. Some are masked, some are mask-less. Not everyone follows the rules! There are few places to escape to where you are not threatened by the noncompliant…I guess it is too much to ask that we care about our fellow humanity!

I pass a young tree that is stunted on the edge of the sidewalk. It's thirsting for air, like the asphyxiated we read about in hospital ICUs. I see clouds, puffier in the sky, that are no longer fractured by exhaust trails, looking more pristine than usual. A pale, scintillating light glows through the dinner bubbles on main street as homeless, vagabonds stroke their beards in homage. Another morning driven by fear, disillusionment, and pots and pans floating in the kitchen sink. The dried up dog urine from the night before wafts through the boardinghouse.

I ponder if my neighbor is shacking up with another spouse while I work remotely, isolated, in the office. The panes are glazed with ice, forming a translucent seal that I can't see through anymore. A news report is broadcasting that a number of whales are dying off the coast of Mexico. What could have caused that? Water pollution? Scarcity of food? Bubble wrap twisted in their lungs? Or a new water-borne virus that came straight from the mainland?

Speaking of which, the home aquarium looks bugged out. Fish that are typically healthy are ill with an unknown infection. Under the microscope it looks round and spiky. I hope that isn't the case.

The new rugs are infested with bed bugs. My maid is afraid to use any vacuum cleaner that does not have a HEPA filter. She insists I buy her one or else she will not clean anything. I'm highly allergic to dust mites so this is an impending disaster.

In other circumstances a cool breeze is welcomed. It is now sinister as it could be carrying dangerous air droplets that could infect the household. I don my mask, oops, my two masks, the surgical one underneath, the cloth one on top, as the NIH Director, Dr. Doom, has recommended. It's hard trying to find a balance where you can breathe and not cause spontaneous cyanosis. Turning blue from oxygen deprivation somehow does not provide me comfort.

In this state of mind, I risk waking every morning. I have these marathon dreams that ramble into nowhere, that take me light years away, then I come back, to my dog yakking in my face. It is no small wonder I can still think straight with all the shit the radio and television announcers spout and the thousand streaming services that feed us propaganda mixed with facts every day. You have to be a magician to understand all the garble, the senseless talking heads, the cacophony of nothingness that smothers our minds. I walk to the coffee shop every morning to rid myself of auditory hysteria *(a new disease)*, to establish some sanity in my life. A respite that is not always precarious and unsettling. As least, in my world of knowing, I can be assured coffee will stimulate me, and wake me up, to another round of blah in this blah waiting period for blah progress.

Someone stops at the door. Uber eats on the way. Must remember to wipe down the package, could be contaminated with *THE VIRUS*. Safe hygiene is always leaking into my mind. Like a runaway train on a mission. I hear cymbals in the background. White noise of my life. I shook violently, the Uber Eats were poisoned. A mass conspiracy to depopulate. They have a contract with the NSA. So says my whacky mailman. I rush to the toilet to empty the Covid remnants of my life. Strange I think like this. To get over the hump, instead of straddling between two worlds, one normal and the other a distortion of what is possible.

Amazing progress are other words for small progress. Multiple vaccines to choose from, but none I qualify for yet. HERD IMMUNITY is like the golden fleece, an impossible quest. The roll-out for the vaccine is like the show BOTCHED. But this reality show we are now living has *head counts*.

The delusions used in language are what are amazing. Hidden behind the words is where meaning actually comes from. I explore meanings. Derivatives from the subconscious coming forward. If we understood our subconscious we would understand our consciousness more of the time. I opine: "comprehension is a noble art", but few of us realize that.

We stroke our own egos in an effort to support what we manifest. We are merely permeable cellular jelly gyrating around in a disinterested universe. We think we are more important than the small tadpoles we see swimming around in a green pond. Most of us prostitute ourselves some way on our jobs. We say "yes" when we mean "no" to keep employed and to give the illusion of peace. Ancillary to the suppository is the right pointer finger! Say that during a performance review! Learn to calibrate language ever so delicately. That will ensure survival!

The slower pace is mesmerizing. Trips to Walmart and the local grocers being the magnum opus of any given day. Virus flies by me every day but I am not cognizant of it. I suspect it is aware of me, looking for a kink in my body's armor. I shoo it away.
 I remind myself again and again to be safe and not to take needless risks. The cashier gives me a subliminal once over, making sure I am not disreputable as I eye the corona tattoo on her exposed left arm. She is not a masterpiece by Leonardo's standards. But cheeky in an attractive way. I blow past the Walmart greeter as he is saying "hello, welcome to Walmart". I feel bad but I must get out quickly. The virus you know.

Everything is falling apart. My mask is sliding off my nose. It has left me with a hyperbolic rash that I can't hide. My eyes itch. I hope no particles of virus have mistakenly taken them for a home. I can smell coffee so I am relieved. I use this as the litmus test for good health. Once I can't smell that I know I am in trouble.

The images of variants percolating in my stomach frazzles me. I shelter myself in my car as I wait for calm to return. Hypnagogic, I struggle to stay awake. I think I have caught the virus, or it has caught me. Snared in another trap. I await my next report in my inbox from *Medical News* to check on my new symptoms. I reach out only to find the station I usually listen to is doing a test on the emergency broadcast system. All the stations are proclaiming stay at home orders, be wary of the virus, distance yourself from yourself, even from the insects in your backyard. New reports link mosquitoes to the Covid-19 virus (not true). As if the West Nile virus was not enough to keep you indoors.

Gone are the days of my carefree life. I routinely triple mask now in public and look like a character from the *Handmaid's Tale*. Ofdan they call me on the street, only my eyes are exposed, surveilling for trouble. I wish it wasn't so, but life in all its charm in a bubble is the new normal.

The metamorphosis is almost complete. Society has changed forever. Cities are being swallowed up and bled of people. The suburbs are filling up, with people fearful of mass transit, crowded conditions, and the lack of space. Remote work is becoming routine as companies find out the cost of real estate and expenses they can shed.

The rails are like ghost towns, even the parkways seem quieter. A great calm has arisen across the land. That is, outside of hospitals, where there is constant noise and sirens, and refrigerated trucks, stark reminders of the pandemic.

I lost an Aunt and a neighbor to this slippery contagion, unseen horror of the masses. Its phantasmagorical nature and invisibility lead us to the false belief we can duck it. I witnessed shouting matches around the value of wearing masks. People dulled by the length of the quarantine taking out their frustrations on any target they seize upon. Survival of the loudest it seems.

The real toll is on our minds. This new reality can exacerbate mental illness allowing vulnerable individuals to unravel, like a serpentine snake coiled and ready to strike in the far recesses of sanity. Government provides hotlines to call, a small allowance that doesn't address the bigger picture of pain and uncertainty this continued pandemic brings.

I step off the sidewalk, filled with dread, a brewing tinnitus has become worse. I need to determine if this is the onset of something. The beginning of the end or maybe a new beginning. It strikes me that each moment of time is becoming more important. Time used to run by, like water, it's meaning transitory. Today, it is different, each action stretches onward into infinity, *rippling into the universe of things and non-things.*

I see a bird house dangerously close to slipping off a branch dangling by my fence. Teetering on the edge, symbolizing the psyche of humanity. I go over and move it to a safer limb. This small act of kindness restores my vitality. An emotional link is formed between the doing and the good deed. A small token of rewilding.

Passerby stragglers brave the cold air to walk their small pooches near where I live. Their plodding reminds me of old camels in the desert searching for an oasis in the sun. Their greeting is heavy from the boredom they are experiencing. I almost want to shout at them to "wake up!" and enjoy the gift of life so many have lost.

No matter how dangerous our environments are, civility should not be overlooked. I notice the sky is turning a deep grey. The weather is turning. I grapple with the beauty of being alive, as tiny snowflakes anoint the landscape with a blanket of fleece.
The virus lingers. So do I.

dramatic lit.

finite things and how they are brought to us
(a performance piece)
煦 (Susie Zhu)

A man in a chair, the middle of the stage, smoking: a white square umbrella held over his head. Another is walking, circling anti-clockwise centrifugal. Distance between increases until he walks out of the stage, sight, sound.

The stage dimly lit and the umbrella almost glowing.

The stage is covered with cigarette butts, smoke,
as he walks, cigarettes pushed along to the outside the darkness out of light, to open up.

When he exits the stage should have been cleared except for a lonely island floating in the center. He should make utterly heavy and slow steps on a regular beat (but no metronome). The smoking man would drop the ends to the ground once he'd finished and light a new one. VOICE 2 should be a male voice.

The space abounds with rain, and the space abounds with silence.

Raining Sound.
(and would persist through out)

VOICE 1: Where do these clouds come from?

(Sound of blowing a balloon, slowly)
the man should be breathing out the smoke simultaneously as the balloon is heard to be blown up.
All the balloons blown up should not be let go before asked to.

VOICE 3: The shadows
VOICE 1: are white,

        stretching out, far

VOICE 2: The idea
VOICE 1: Far low east, drowning into the ocean…/
VOICE 3: (OVERLAPPING) They are here—they are coming—

VOICE 1: into   dissipation   of contours   white

as of an after image

white
as a color   unliable to the eye
VOICE 3:   to the valves

VOICE 2: the one we do not know.

Raining Sound.

VOICE 1: Check,   ah, ah—
VOICE 3: (Say Ah— in a comfortably low voice to the longest duration possible, yes, until the very last breathe. Say another Ah as soon as VOICE 1 speaks again. Repeat until new instruction)

VOICE 2: Another sun has melt away,
VOICE 1: Draw another line,
VOICE 2: Horizon?
VOICE 1: Yes, repeat, shall we call it another day?

Raining Sound. Ah Sound from VOICE 3
(VOICE 2 can join VOICE 3 with the AH-ing whenever he likes)

VOICE 1: Listen

(VOICE 3 stop saying AH)

VOICE 3: Burning sounds. / VOICE 2: (OVERLAPPING) What is a day?

VOICE 1: Let's begin with facing a sound,
VOICE 3: Stop swimming, stop breathing, stop
VOICE 1: lie down on your wrist, you'll hear your own veins
VOICE 3: A ancient chant   What does it say?/
VOICE 1:   (OVERLAPPING) Louder, the sound has

to be louder, than your own diverging streams, streaming—

VOICE 3:   Do not get carried away!
VOICE 1: face it, stare into it, into, its eyes

when you find the eyes, it should be close

VOICE 3: close

VOICE 1: to the border. Wide enough. Remember—

VOICE 2:   walking down a road still under construction
                                                a lightless early night, half chopped asphalt,
                                                half embraced air, imagining

                                                                    himself

                                        chased down by the weathering of — /

VOICE 1:   (OVERLAPPING) that's the size of a day,

roughly.

VOICE 3: And you draw another line
VOICE 2: (Sound of blowing a balloon, slowly, keep blowing until VOICE 1 finishes the next speech)

Raining Sound.

VOICE 1: It is nothing alien. Remember?
            we were all once in a rain, heavy pouring, dark suffocating,

VOICE 3: Boundless, the rain, raining on forever that it becomes solidification

VOICE 1:   Annihilation—Boundless, seamless.

                                    And we are lost, annulled, incarcerated. And we

have to,

(the sitting man lowers the umbrella gradually until he could no more.)

VOICE 2: (Gasp deeply to recharge air) Breath
VOICE 1:   (OVERLAPPING) Break
VOICE 3:   (OVERLAPPING) Braid

VOICE 2:   Break
VOICE 3: (OVERLAPPING) Breath
VOICE 1: (OVERLAPPING) Braid, braid them thinly

VOICE 3: carefully
VOICE 1: into trenches, flow with an expanding scheme shaped

VOICE 1: like grids/
VOICE 3: (OVERLAPPING) like a vessel

VOICE 2: Clocks

VOICE 1:   are lies. Time never runs like that.
VOICE 2: It flows   off

VOICE 1:   as we made it visible, durable, a river

                                        —to sail away.

VOICE 3: (mumbles in an extremely tiny voice, persist until new instructions)

What is river, if not a fragment of sea?
What is river, if not a fragment of sea?
What is river, if not a fragment of sea?
What is river, if not a fragment of sea?
....

The smoking man tosses his umbrella aside gently, facing-up, like a paper boat.

Raining Sound and VOICE 3's barely audible chanting.

VOICE 3: Where is the
VOICE 1: Quiet, they are watching—
VOICE 3: Eyes?

VOICE 1: They see.

       They see perfection in the guise of desire   sitting

       in what we've concocted.

VOICE 3: Beneath
VOICE 2: Turtles?

VOICE 1: Like them but not...turtles,

    they march,

VOICE 3: too slowly, like turtles, almost.

VOICE 1: And too white, the shadows, hiding the world behind.

Shadows articulate to shadows, neither heard and both distant throbbing, pounding on their,

VOICE 3: they,
VOICE 1: so they start their infinite escape
VOICE 3: winding
VOICE 1:   back on the

VOICE 2: Clock
VOICE 3:   But time never runs that way!

VOICE 1: Turtles,

        oh, they make me sad. They are too slow,

                to return to themselves

VOICE 3: ——before time runs out into the sky

                    or evaporates.

(All the balloons blown up are let gone)
Drastic Balloon Decease Sound.

The cigarette ends on the stage has been all cleaned off (except for the most centered circular area where the smoking man sits) by the walking man as he reached the very edge. The walking man exits.

The smoking man come off the chair, takes the cigarette his smoking and started to draw lines around him using it, he moves strictly like a compass, turning around with his arm froze in the initial pose.

Raining Sound.

VOICE 1: We all share the desire to overpower time, that's what make us human.

We made our effort,

VOICE 2: Lines—
VOICE 3:   some are effortless.   draw, drown, draw, drown...

(VOICE 3 starts chanting in a tiny voice, imitating a clock sound)

VOICE 1: (Ignoring VOICE 3)

                some are more effective, and we preserve them.

VOICE 2: branching—

VOICE 1: Smoking as consuming, and dreaming, depositing.
VOICE 2: Slowly, clotting—

(VOICE 3 stops)
VOICE 3: Do you smoke?

VOICE 1: to de-dream something, may be the best way to husk time.
Smokers, leave the ends in your dream. When you head back to retrieve, they'd weave you an atlas, so you won't need to bear the silence again.

VOICE 2: I do...and I don't. I smoke only in my dreams.

VOICE 1: wipe down, white—
VOICE 3: (with very low voice)   down, the stairs, twisting

backwards, deep

      down below to the most perplexing sea dark

like the dark soft rock of water pre-conception dark

embodiment   beyond knowledge
dark that   gives birth

exists to efface

VOICE 1: efface to exist

(distracted by VOICE 3, but throughout the rest, speaks as if in its own world)
    washing

VOICE 3: away, away with them in
VOICE 1: for the new eyes to listen, to light, running past,
VOICE 3:   (OVERLAPPING) toward the past

VOICE 1:   running through
VOICE 3: you, veins,
VOICE 1:

      resting in immense nest of water, time impasto.

VOICE 2: Eyes?
VOICE 3: draw
VOICE 2: drown
VOICE 3: draw
VOICE 2: drown
(the clock sound persist)
...

VOICE 1: (right after the first "draw" by VOICE 3) them,

eyes,
eyes, cracks   a   towards,
beyond all the drifting
penumbra, make it a container

find eyes,
you'll find

border,
the end, ends   —bring the ends,
          they deceive rain, a mirror,
                        and alibi,

you'll hear true voice

of time,
only through seeing

reclaim   sight   of the intangible,
                                        lines,
    slower   than the eternal, surpassing

physicality
climb in,

like the moon does to a day,
like a day being diffused,

being diffused...

VOICE 3: draw
VOICE 2: drown

VOICE 3: draw
VOICE 2: drown
....

The smoking man is still drawing circles, the clock sound persist.
The performance could end at any point, preferably never.

writing tips.

writing tips from editors.

*Journal daily- developing a habit of writing casually will help you learn more about your voice.
*Read, A LOT! The best writers are frequent readers.
*Find a critique partner (see our interview with Joanne Rock to learn more.)
*Write for yourself first. What do you need? What do you want discover? About yoursel? The world?
*Re-read often. Put yourself in the position of your reader. Is it still clear? Is it still engaging? Are their pieces of story/character in your head that never made it to the page?

writing challenge.

*Write uniterrupted for 10 minutes a day.
*Foward moving only!
*Write something fundamentally different than anything you've written before (genre, form, etc.) Experiment!
*See what you have after a month. (And submit it to the next issue of Bloom!)

writing prompts.

*Write something inspired by a color palette.
*Write something inspired by a landscape.
*Write something that starts with a door opening.
*Write something that includes a change of light.
*Write something that starts with a breeze.
*Write something that includes a fruit or vegetable.
*Write something from the perspective of a historical figure.
*Wrtie something from the perspective of someone who doesn't exist yet.
*Write something that includes at least 3 moments of prolonged eye contact.
*Write something where the characters can't see each other.
*Write something from the prespective of a body part.
*Write something that contains a whisper.

whats new.

publishing opportunites.

*Tradition & Hybrid Publishing Opportunties at Red Penguin Books
- For full-length manuscripts only
-Go to redpenguinbooks.com/book-publishing or email stephanie@redpenguinbooks.com to find more information!
-<u>Deadline</u>: rolling

*The Red Penguin Collection
-An anthology collection for short form work.
-Each collection focuses on a different theme or genre, ranging from mystery and romance to coming of age stories & social topics.
-Submit up to 5000 words of short stories, essays, plays, or excerpts.
-No cost!
-Go to redpenguinbooks.com/the-red-penguin-collection/ or email thepenguincollection@gmail.com to find more information!
-<u>Deadline</u>: specific to individual anthologies

*Bloom- Issue 3
-Another edition of Bloom, a literary magazine dedicated to the growth of the emerging author.
-Submit up to 1500 words of short stories, essays, plays or excerpts
-No cost!
-Go to redpenguinbook.com/bloom-lit-magazine or email bloomlitmagazine@gmail.com to find more information!
-<u>Deadline</u>: June 15, 2021

selling on six continents

promotional opportunities

Video Book Trailer & Audiobooks:
*Visit www.redpenguinbooks.com to find rates and past work.

Sign up to be a Guest Author on "Between the Covers":
*Promote your book on publisher Stephanie Larkin's talk show.
*Visit https://betweenthecoverstv.com/be-our-guest/ to sign up!

educational opportunities

Classes With Open Registration:
*Marketing Your Book with Publisher Stephanie Larkin
*Poetry Workshop with Award-Winning Poet Linda Trott Dickman
*Creative Writing Course with Author Margreit Maitland

Coming Up Soon:
*Editing Your Manuscript!
*How to Self-Publish Your Book
*The HowToDoIts for WhoDoneits: Mystery Writer's Class

To find more information visit https://redpenguinclasses.com/

www.ingramcontent.com/pod-product-compliance
Lightning Source LLC
Chambersburg PA
CBHW082207090526
44583CB00021BA/2841